a Wee Guide to

Prehistoric Scotland

Scottish Crannog Centre, Kenmore

a Wee Guide to
Prehistoric Scotland

Ann MacSween

GOBLINSHEAD

Musselburgh

a Wee Guide to Prehistoric Scotland

© Ann MacSween and Martin Coventry 1999
Published by **GOBLINSHEAD**
130B Inveresk Road
Musselburgh EH21 7AY
Scotland
tel 0131 665 2894; *fax* 0131 653 6566; *email* goblinshead@sol.co.uk

All rights reserved. No part of this book may be reproduced, stored in an
information retrieval system, or transmitted in any form or by any means,
mechanical or electrical, photocopied or recorded, without the express
permission of the publishers except for review or educational purposes.

British Library Cataloguing in Publication Data
A catalogue record for this book is available from the British Library.

ISBN 1 899874 23 2

Typeset by **GOBLINSHEAD** using Desktop Publishing

WEE GUIDES

William Wallace
The Picts
Scottish History
The Jacobites
Robert Burns
Mary, Queen of Scots
Robert the Bruce
Haunted Castles of Scotland
Old Churches and Abbeys of Scotland
Castles and Mansions of Scotland
New for 1999
Prehistoric Scotland
Macbeth and Early Scotland
Whisky
Also published
The Castles of Scotland 2E (£14.50)
Haunted Places of Scotland (£7.50)
The Hebrides (£5.95)
William Wallace – Champion of Scotland (£6.95)

a Wee Guide to
Prehistoric Scotland

Contents

List of Illustrations

Acknowledgements

Many thanks to the following people who have provided illustrations for this guide: Martin Coventry (page 2, 10, 14, 16, 19, 20, 21, 30, 37, 40, 42, 44, 48, 52, 56, 59, 60, 64, 66, 67, 78, 80, 86, 89, 100, 108); Trevor Cowie (page 70); Marie Hindmarsh (pages 9, 81); Fraser Hunter (39, 49, 68, 93, 98, 103); Jim Killgore (page 24, 63, 65); Dave Reed (pages 6, 26, 45, 50, 54, 74, 84, 91, 95, 96) and Caroline Wickham-Jones (page 99, 105).

Thanks also to Martin Coventry, Joyce Miller and Hilary Brown of Goblinshead and to Jim Killgore for their help with this volume.

How to Use this Book

This book is divided into two sections:

- The first section (pages 1-29) summarises what is known about the early peoples of Scotland, under the periods Mesolithic (pages 4-5), Neolithic (pages 6-17), Bronze Age (pages 18-22) and Iron Age (pages 23-29).
- The second section (pages 31-115) lists more than 120 prehistoric sites and museums which can be visited. The section begins with maps (pages 32-34) which locate every site, and there is also a list of all the individual sites (page 35-36). The gazetteer is listed alphabetically by location (from page 37). Each entry begins with the name of the site, its location, grid reference and Ordnance Survey Landranger Sheet and its reference on the map (pages 32-34). This is followed by a description of the site then by opening times with contact information and facilities where available. Admission charges are as follows: £ = £3.50 or under; ££ = £3.50-£5.00; £££ = more than £5.00. Some museums with significant archaeological displays are listed after this section (pages 109-115).

An index concludes the book (pages 116-118).

Warning

While the information in this book was believed to be correct at time of going to press – and was checked, where possible, with the visitor attractions – opening times and facilities, or other information, may differ from that included. All information should be checked with the visitor attractions before embarking on any journey. Inclusion in the text is no indication whatsoever that a site is open to the public or that it should be visited.

Inclusion or exclusion of any site should not be considered as a comment or judgement on that site.

Locations on the map are approximate.

Preface

The upstanding prehistoric monuments presented in this guide represent 4000 years of life on the land we now know as Scotland. The lack of written texts for the period means that archaeologists depend on the interpretation of ancient monuments and evidence from excavations and survey work to gain an understanding of the life of those who built and used the sites.

In any guide to Prehistoric Scotland there are about 60 sites such as Skara Brae and Callanish which will always appear. Beyond these there are a large number of interesting sites and it is a matter of personal choice which to include.

Some areas of Scotland have a greater number of surviving upstanding monuments than others. The use of stone for building in regions such as Orkney and Shetland has resulted in better preservation than in the south where timber and turf were more often used. Centuries of intensive agriculture have also taken a toll in many regions. This is not to say that sites in these areas are any less interesting or important – but this is a guide to 'visible' archaeology.

For those whose appetite is whetted by reading this book there is an abundance of literature - some of the more general introductions are listed on the following page and they in turn will point the reader to studies of a more period-specific or region-specific nature.

I hope that you will enjoy this guide – visiting these sites will also take you to some of Scotland's most spectacular areas. Please respect the monuments and the countryside.

AMacS, Edinburgh, May 1999

Further Reading

Armit, I 1998 *Scotland's Hidden History*. (Tempus).

Armit, I 1997 *Celtic Scotland*. (Batsford).

Ashmore, PJ 1996 *Neolithic and Bronze Age Scotland*. (Batsford).

Barclay, G 1998 *Farmers, Temples and Tombs*. (Canongate).

Edwards, K and Ralston, IBM 1997 *Scotland: environment and archaeology*. (Wiley).

Finlayson, B 1998 *Wild Harvesters*. (Canongate).

Hingley, R 1998 *Settlement and Sacrifice*. (Canongate).

MacSween, A 1989 *Prehistoric Scotland*. (Batsford).

Ritchie, A and Ritchie, JNG 1981 *Scotland: archaeology and early history*. (Edinburgh University Press).

Wickham-Jones, C 1994 *Scotland's First Settlers*. (Batsford).

a Wee Guide to
Prehistoric
Scotland

Introduction

Introduction

The period covered by this book stretches from 4000 BC to the first few centuries AD, a time span divided by archaeologists into three periods – the Neolithic, Bronze Age and Iron Age. Dates quoted in the text are approximate and derive from the radiocarbon dating of sites and artefacts. The labels Neolithic, Bronze Age and Iron Age are a convenient shorthand when discussing the major changes observable in the archaeological record. In effect change would have been very gradual and its pace would have varied from one area to another.

The Neolithic period, 4000 BC to 2000 BC, is the period of the first farmers, characterised by communal monuments – cursus, henges and stone circles – as much as by domestic settlements. One of the major changes noted in excavated sites of the Bronze Age, 2000 BC to 700 BC, is a shift of emphasis to the individual, reflected in single burials. The Bronze Age is also, of course, marked by the beginnings of metalworking, the use of bronze for tools and weapons which implies systems for trading either raw materials or finished products. The Iron Age, 700 BC to the first few centuries AD, is characterised by the introduction of iron technology, but also by an increase in the building of defensive settlements and enclosures – a trend which had started in the late Bronze Age.

Scotland's archaeological record, however, begins in the Mesolithic, the period which preceded the Neolithic.

Mesolithic

The earliest evidence of human occupation in Scotland is from the Mesolithic period. Settlement sites of hunter-gatherer communities date back 10,000 years, after the last glaciation. By this time human groups had been living intermittently in Britain for about 500,000 years and it is probable that there was earlier occupation in Scotland too, its traces obliterated by subsequent glaciations.

Mesolithic sites have been found in many parts of Scotland as far north as Orkney. The hunter-gatherer groups which occupied them inhabited a country which was largely covered in woodland. The Mesolithic people hunted such animals as wild pig and red and roe deer, caught birds and fished, and gathered nuts, fruit and shellfish. Recent evidence from excavations on Colonsay, where a huge pit of hazelnut shells was uncovered, indicates that the Mesolithic groups on the island were managing the hazel trees as well as collecting. Environmental evidence from other areas points to the burning of woodland, perhaps to establish clearings which would have encouraged a particular type of tree to grow, or wild animals to graze.

The Mesolithic tool kit included implements formed from bone, antler, flint and stone. Tiny flint blades or microliths characterise the period. These blades would have been hafted to wooden shafts to form barbs and cutting edges. Bone tools recovered include harpoons and fish hooks. Another characteristic tool of the Mesolithic in Scotland is the 'limpet scoop', a small shovel-like implement made of stone, bone or antler which, it has been suggested, was used to prise limpets from the rocks.

Occupation sites of the Mesolithic groups are

commonly found along Scotland's coasts and rivers. On the island of Rum, pits, postholes and charcoal from hearths as well as the probable floor outline of a tent were uncovered during recent excavations. While some sites such as the settlement on Rum indicate at least semi-permanency, other sites may represent more temporary occupation. There are, for example, seashore midden sites of various sizes comprising shells and stone and bone tools which may represent short-lived or seasonal food processing camps. One of the largest is on the island of Oronsay. Traces of Mesolithic occupation are also found in caves and rock shelters. Evidence suggests that these hunter-gatherer groups moved from one area to another depending on the resources available in a particular season.

Both the location of Mesolithic sites (along shores and river banks) and the abundance of excavated fish bones suggest the use of boats such as dugout canoes, or perhaps wooden-framed, skin-covered coracles although no examples have yet been found.

Neolithic

The first evidence for farming in Britain dates from
around 4000 BC. The shift from a hunter-gather
economy to farming would have been a gradual one.
Hunting, fishing and gathering no doubt contributed
much to the early Neolithic economy. In some areas
groups of hunter-gatherers existing alongside early
farming communities. Sheep, goats, pigs, cattle and
dogs were the early domesticates and wheat and
naked and six-row barley were the first crops grown
by the Neolithic farmers. Much of the clearance of
Scotland's woodland was carried out at this time with
large areas being deforested to establish fields in the
late Neolithic.

Settlements
The early farmers lived either in farmsteads, probably
occupied by one or two families, such as the double
building at **Knap of Howar,** Papa Westray or the house
at **Pettigarth's Field**, Shetland. Later there is evidence

Skara Brae

for small communities, as at **Skara Brae** and **Barnhouse**, Orkney Mainland. Some of the larger buildings such as the **Stanydale** 'temple' on Shetland Mainland may have been used as communal meeting places. In the north where stone was used for building, the sites have survived well – at **Skara Brae** the stone furniture was still in place when the blown sand was cleared from the houses. Traces of field systems survive in some of the more remote areas as at **Scord of Brouster,** Shetland Mainland, where the remains of stone-built field walls can be easily made out. Further south, where timber rather than stone was used in house-building, and subsequent architecture has been more intense, the traces of Neolithic settlements are more difficult to detect, but many sites are known, their outlines often identified from aerial photographs. Excavations at Balbridie, Aberdeenshire, for example, uncovered the remains of a 24 m long timber building which was radiocarbon dated to the Neolithic – around 3900-3700 BC. This house seems too large for a single family but may have housed an extended family or been used as a communal structure for families living in the area. No similar buildings have yet been found anywhere else in Britain.

In central and southern Scotland are a group of enclosures, identified on aerial photographs, which have been ringed by substantial timber fences. One example, at Meldon Bridge in the Borders, has been excavated and was found to have pits and postholes inside, indicating domestic occupation, although whether the fencing represents early fortification or was constructed purely for effect is a matter for speculation.

A wide range of artefacts has been recovered from Neolithic sites in Scotland. Flint continued to be used and was fashioned into arrowheads, knives and axes – there is evidence for large-scale flint extraction during the Neolithic at the Buchan gravels in Aberdeenshire. 'Prestige' artefacts such as polished stone axes, many of which are too small and too finely finished for practical work, often derive from sources remote from the site of discovery and are indicative of trade or gift-giving. Larger 'everyday' items such as ards and hammerstones were probably made from whatever stone was available locally. The Neolithic also marks the beginning of pottery production in Scotland. The earliest vessels were hand-built with coils of clay. Round-based forms with a decorated collar were amongst the early forms, with bucket shaped, elaborately decorated 'Grooved Ware' being introduced later. As well as domestic artefacts there is also evidence for personal adornment – shell and bone beads were, for example, found at **Skara Brae**.

For the Neolithic communities ceremony and ritual would have been integral to the tasks of their daily lives. In an economy where a season of bad weather could lead to crop failure and all its associated problems, offerings to the gods at appropriate points in the yearly calendar would have been important, and it is probable that the gods would also have been thanked for a good harvest. Events such as birth and death would have been marked in the community just as they are today. In Scotland there are many ceremonial and ritual sites dating to the Neolithic.

Tombs
Scotland's Neolithic communities housed their dead in communal tombs, part of a tradition of tomb-building found throughout the west of Europe and lasting from the early fourth millennium BC to the mid third millennium BC. Some of the tombs have survived better than others. Stone cairns provided a handy source of building material for later inhabitants and in some cases like **Cairnholy I and II,** Kirkcudbright,

mounds have been almost completely robbed, leaving only the larger stones of the passage and chamber in position, or structures have been built into the mound as at the **Mutiny Stones**, East Lothian – in this case a sheep fank.

The tombs were designed so that they could be reopened for a new burial. In general there is a central chamber, often reached by a passage, which is covered by a large cairn or mound. At unexcavated sites, such as **Dun Bharpa**, Barra, it is often impossible to determine the structure of the tomb. Within the catch-all classification 'chambered tomb' there is a great deal of diversity. Designs vary from simple forms with a short passage leading to a small chamber, such as **Unival**, North Uist, to more elaborate forms such as

Midhowe, Rousay, which has a 23 m long chamber divided into twelve compartments, or the double-storey chamber of **Taversoe Tuick** also on Rousay. Their builders seem to have managed to express their individuality, while keeping within the bounds of what was considered acceptable by the community. An

Maes Howe – see next page

example of this individuality is the triangular arrangement of stones on the exterior of the mound at **Blackhammer**, Rousay in Orkney. The standard of building observable in some of the tombs is testament to the great architectural and engineering skills of their builders. One cannot but marvel at the craftsmanship reflected in some of the later Neolithic tombs such as **Maes Howe,** Orkney Mainland, and **Quoyness**, Sanday.

Some of the design aspects of the tombs are specific to a particular geographic area. Maes Howe tombs are only found on Orkney. They have a narrow passage leading to a rectangular or square chamber, from which lead side cells. Examples include Maes Howe and **Wideford**, both on the Orkney Mainland. Other sites like the cairn at **Auchagallon**, Arran, which appears to incorporate a small stone circle, and the **Dwarfie Stane**, Hoy, a rock-cut tomb with a passage and two chambers, have no parallels and must be put down to the creativity or genius of the designer.

A further group of tombs dating to the Neolithic are long barrows and long cairns. Long barrows have a

Auchagallon

turf and stone mound (eg **Capo**, Kincardine) whereas long cairns have a stone cairn (eg **Cnoc Freiceadain**, Caithness). Few excavations have been carried out but on excavated sites such as Lochhill, Kirkcudbright, evidence of timber mortuary structures has been found under the mound. Sometimes earlier cairns were incorporated under the mound as at Camster Long Cairn (**Grey Cairns of Camster**), Caithness, where the stone mound incorporated two separate round mounds.

The rituals carried out at these tombs must be a matter of speculation but where excavations have been carried out, some clues have emerged. The arrangement of the human remains within the chambers indicates that bodies were not placed in a chamber and then left undisturbed, but that there was a lot of rearranging of the bones, perhaps before a new burial. At **Isbister**, South Ronaldsay, the bones seemed to have been arranged according to type, with many of the skulls placed in two of the side cells. Discoveries such as this have led to the suggestion that the remains were disarticulated before being placed in the tombs, perhaps after exposure on a mortuary platform. At **Unival**, North Uist, piles of bones and pottery indicate the clearing of the chamber between burials and it is possible that material was removed from the chamber as well as added to it. This treatment of the remains indicates that the dead were treated as part of the communal ancestors rather than as individuals.

Small artefacts such as bone beads have been recovered from the chambers and these probably represent personal decorations and possessions. Pottery and animal bones have also been found, for example in the chamber at Unstan, Orkney Mainland, where the remains of at least 30 round-based, shallow bowls were found. These most likely represent food offerings, perhaps to appease the gods. A high number of bones of one type would suggest that a certain animal or bird held a special significance to a community and was perhaps regarded as a totem. At **Cuween**, Orkney Mainland, the skulls of 24 dogs were found and at **Isbister**, South Ronaldsay, the chamber contained the remains of at least ten white-tailed sea eagles.

Many of the chambers would only have enabled a small number of people to enter the tomb at one time and forecourts like those at **Barpa Langass**, North Uist, and **Rubh' an Dunain**, Skye, may have provided a stage for burial rituals which could be observed by a greater number of individuals than could have been involved if the rituals were carried out in the chamber. The theory that the forecourts were used in this way is strengthened by excavated evidence. At **Cairnholy I**, Kirkcudbright, for example, traces of six fires were found in the forecourt as well as a broken pot.

Many of the tombs appear to have been deliberately sealed after the final burial in a tomb, possibly an attempt to contain the spirit of the tomb. At **Midhowe**, Rousay, the entrance was sealed with stone walling and the roof opened and filled with stony debris, while at **Cairnholy I**, Kirkcudbright, the space between the portal stones was built up with slabs and a large 'closing stone' leaned up against the sealed entrance. The forecourt was covered by a layer of earth and small stones and then slabs were piled on top.

As well as having a burial function, many of the chambered tombs would have been visible from a distance and important to the community in defining their territory. The tiny Orkney island of **Holm of Papa Westray,** for example, has two tombs which may mark the territories of two communities, one living at the north of the island, one living at the south.

Standing stones and henges

A new range of communal monuments, presumably
with ritual or ceremonial function, was constructed in
the later Neolithic, during the third millennium BC.
Many of the stone circles, standing stones and
alignments date to the Early Bronze Age but will be
discussed together, as without excavation their dating
is problematic. Stone circles and henges were often
built in spectacular settings and even today many
continue to dominate the landscape. Over the years
most of the standing stones and stone circles have been
incorporated into local folklore. The stones at **Lundin
Links**, Fife, are said to mark the graves of Danish
warriors defeated by Macbeth, while those at
Strontoiller, Oban, are believed to mark the resting
place of the Irish hero Diarmid. Some stones are
reputed to have a ritual function. The holed stone at
Ballymeanoch, Kilmartin Glen, is said to have been
used for sealing contracts including marriage contracts
– the parties would join hands through the hole in the
stone.

Stone circles are found in all parts of Scotland with
concentrations in the north-east, the south-west, and
the Outer Hebrides and were probably meeting places
for rituals and ceremonies. There is a great range of
styles. In many cases the eventual appearance of a
circle is largely dictated by the local geology ranging
from the squat granite boulders of the **Torhouse** circle,
Wigtown, to the slim pillars of Lewisian gneiss which
make up the **Callanish** circle on Lewis. Other factors
such as the size of the circle or the number of stones
would have been the choice of the community. There is
a great variety in size. At the smaller end of the scale
are circles such as **Lochbuie**, Mull while the **Twelve
Apostles**, Dumfries, at 88 m in diameter, is the largest
circle in Scotland and the fifth largest in Britain. The
number of stones also varies greatly, from circles with

under ten stones to the circle of **Pobull Fhinn,** North Uist, which originally had 48 stones, and the **Ring of Brodgar** on Orkney, which had 60.

In addition to the stone circles there are a number of other settings of standing stones in Caithness: including a horse-shoe-shaped arrangement at **Achavanich** and a fan-shaped setting, known as the **Hill o' Many Stanes**, which probably originally comprised 600 stones. Single stones are also common throughout Scotland, some of the tallest being **Ballinaby**, Islay, which is almost 5 m high and **Clach an Trushal**, Lewis, which is 6 m high. Such stones may have marked meeting places for members of the surrounding community.

As with the chambered tombs there is some regional variation, the recumbent stone circles of the north-east perhaps being the best known group. These circles incorporate a prostrate or recumbent stone with an upright, or flanker, on each side. While most of the circles conform to this general layout there is some variation such as at **Easter Aquorthies,** Inverurie,

Easter Aquorthies

where two blocks of stone are set at right angles to the recumbent, facing into the interior of the circle and may have delineated a ceremonial area. The recumbent and flankers are sometimes further defined by choosing a different type of stone to that used for the remaining stones. At **Sunhoney**, Banchory, the recumbent is of grey granite and the uprights are of red granite, while at **Tomnaverie,** Aboyne, the circle is again of red granite and the recumbent is of whinstone.

An astronomical function has been suggested for the stone circles and alignments. **Callanish** stone circle on Lewis, for example, has been interpreted as a lunar observatory, while measurements carried out at the site of **Kintraw**, Kilmartin, purport to show that the site was used to mark the mid-winter solstice by sighting onto a notch in the Paps of Jura. The recumbents have been interpreted as being placed in the position at which the moon rose or set at the major standstill if viewed from within the circle.

While stone circles are found in other parts of Western Europe, henges are a group of monuments found only in Britain. A henge is a circular earthwork comprising a bank and ditch, the bank being on the exterior of the ditch. Entry into the central area was by way of a causeway across the ditch and a passage through the bank. Some henges have two, opposed, entrances. The distribution of henges is largely east-coast, with the exception of the north-east where the recumbent stone circles may have formed a similar role. Several of the henges have a stone circle within the central area and evidence for timber circles has been uncovered on some excavated sites. During excavations at **Balfarg Henge**, Fife, evidence for a timber circle and at least one stone circle was found and at **Cairnpapple**, West Lothian, excavation revealed that there had been a circle of 24 stones within the henge.

Henges are generally interpreted as meeting places for the local communities and where excavation has been carried out evidence suggests ritual feasting or offerings. At the **Stones of Stenness**, Orkney Mainland, the sheep and cattle bones found in the ditch were identified as largely the extremities of limbs, probably the remains of joints of meat.

In some areas the concentration of ritual and burial sites leads to the conclusion that these are special locations perhaps representing the focus for a number of communities over generations. The area taking in the **Stones of Stenness**, **Maes Howe** and the **Ring of Brodgar** on Orkney Mainland would be one such focus, and there are others such as the concentrations of stone circles at **Callanish**, Lewis, and **Machrie Moor**, Arran, or the burial and ritual monuments of Kilmartin Glen which include **Temple Wood** and the **Nether Largie** tombs.

Machrie Moor

Ceremonial Avenues
Also linked to ritual are the cursus monuments of which there are around 30 examples in Scotland. A cursus is a pair of long ditches with the soil usually

banked on the inner edge. The only one which is still upstanding is the **Cleaven Dyke**, Perthshire, part of which has recently been excavated. These sites have been interpreted as ceremonial ways along which participants would process. The Cleaven Dyke is over 2 km long and was built in 34 segments, perhaps over a number of years. The first element on the site was an oval burial mound. This was extended to form a long mound after which the cursus, comprising a pair of widely spaced ditches with a central bank, was added.

Bronze Age

Metalworking was introduced to Scotland just before 2000 BC. For a community used to fashioning their tools from stone, witnessing the manufacture of a copper or bronze object must have been awe-inspiring, and early smiths would have earned the respect, and perhaps even the fear, of the communities they visited. The copper ore was smelted by heating it to over 1000 degrees centigrade. The resulting metal would be cooled and later remelted in a crucible and poured into a mould to make a tool or ornament.

While Scotland has natural deposits of copper, the tin needed to make a bronze object most likely derived from Devon and Cornwall. Many of the gold items from the period are thought to have come from Ireland. Trade, either of finished articles or raw materials, is thus implied and it is probable that only those who had items or services to offer in exchange would have had access to these goods.

Burials
The Bronze Age also marks a change from communal graves to single cremations or inhumations. This points to an increase in the importance of the individual over the collective. Some of the graves of the period contain Beakers, a new type of vessel introduced to Scotland around the same time as bronze working. Beakers are found on sites in many parts of northern and western Europe. They are relatively small, long-necked, vessels and are often decorated with bands of designs. It is thought that Beakers had been placed in the graves full of food or drink. Other personal items such as archery equipment (flint arrowheads and wrist guards) or ornaments (including beads, bangles and earrings) are sometimes

found with these burials. Another type of pottery known as Food Vessels – narrow-based, decorated vessels – is also found accompanying Bronze Age burials. Cremation was common in the Bronze Age, with the burnt bone sometimes being placed in a pit and covered with a large upturned pottery urn.

Many of these burials were made in cists or pits, sometimes within the boundaries of existing henges and stone circles. There are also examples of cremation cemeteries like the one at **Loanhead of Daviot,** Inverurie, where over 30 cremations were buried in a circular enclosure, and the group of burial cairns enclosed by a stone circle at **Cullerlie**, Westhill. Some burials were covered with a massive cairn presumably reflecting the status of the individual or individuals. The cairn on the top of **Tinto Hill**, Biggar, is one of the largest, measuring 45 m in diameter. A mound of similar size, composed largely of earth, was excavated at North Mains, Tayside, and found to have one or more burials in a fenced area under the centre of the mound. Some of the larger cairns are set within Neolithic ceremonial sites. At **Cairnpapple**, West

Clava Cairns – see next page

Lothian, for example, a cairn 15 m in diameter was built inside the henge and later expanded to take in the ditch of the henge, while the **Nether Largie South** chambered tomb in Kilmartin Glen was covered by a Bronze Age cist.

Nether Largie South

As with the Neolithic period, some types of burial monument are restricted to one area of Scotland. One such group is the Clava cairns which are grouped around Inverness. The type site, **Clava Cairns**, also known as Balnuaran of Clava, near Inverness, and the site of **Corrimony,** Glen Urquhart, show the main features of the group – an outer kerb and inner chamber built of large stones and a circle of standing stones surrounding the tomb. When the Corrimony tomb was excavated, a soil stain on the floor of the chamber indicated that one body had been placed in the tomb.

Cup and ring carvings

Cup and ring markings, although difficult to date, are thought to have been carved in the late Neolithic or Bronze Age. They have been found on some standing stones, such as **Ballymeanoch**, and on cist covers, including **Nether Largie North**, both in Kilmartin

Cup and Ring Marks, Kilmichael Glassary

Glen. Rock outcrops were also decorated, usually horizontal outcrops such as at **Achnabreck** and **Cairnbaan**, Kilmartin Glen, and **High Banks**, Kirkcudbright, although one spectacular example of carving on a vertical face recently came to light at **Ballochmyle** in Ayrshire. The greatest concentrations of decorated outcrops are in the west, in Argyll and in Dumfries and Galloway. Despite a number of studies we are no nearer a consensus on their function. Were they purely decorative, or connected with ritual? We may never know.

Settlement

During the Bronze Age, settlement patterns shifted to include upland areas, perhaps because of population pressure in low-lying areas. Various domestic settlements of the period have been excavated, including one near Lairg in Sutherland where a number of round timber houses dating to the early Bronze Age were found. In the south of Scotland the characteristic Bronze Age domestic site is the 'unenclosed platform settlement', a group of hut platforms, the flattened areas on which round houses would have been built. Some Neolithic sites were occupied into the Bronze Age – at **Scord of Brouster**, Shetland, for example, the farm was occupied from around 3000 BC to 1500 BC, although not necessarily continuously.

Another monument type thought to date mainly to the Bronze Age is the burnt mound – a pile of fire-cracked stones and ash. Only a few burnt mounds have been excavated, including the mound of **Liddle**, South Ronaldsay. A building was found under the mound with a hearth in a recess and a large stone trough in the middle of the floor. It is thought that the trough was filled with water into which hot stones were dropped until the water boiled. Food would then have been cooked in the boiling water. An alternative suggestion is that the burnt mounds were saunas or bath-houses.

In the later part of the Bronze Age many more settlements were enclosed or fortified. A deterioration in climate (increased rainfall and a drop in the annual average temperature) probably caused farming in the marginal upland areas to fail, leading in turn to increased pressure on the low-lying areas. The range and amount of weaponry in circulation also increased around this time suggesting a greater emphasis on defence. Among the weapons dating to the later Bronze Age are swords and spears. Such objects are often found in hoards deposited in rivers, lochs and boggy areas, such as that found in Duddingston Loch, Edinburgh, in the eighteenth century. Similar evidence from other parts of Britain and Ireland indicates that these are ritual deposits.

Iron Age

The techniques of iron working were introduced into Scotland around 700 BC. Iron ore could be extracted in many parts of the country and so the trade networks established during the Bronze Age were no longer needed. It is probable, however, that control of the best sources of iron ore would have been maintained by the minority. Competition between neighbouring communities for control of these resources could be one reason for the accelerated trend towards enclosing and defending sites which began in the late Bronze Age. We know very little about the ritual and burial practices of the Iron Age communities and most of the sites of the period are domestic and defensive sites.

Ritual and burial

There is paucity of evidence to give us an accurate picture of the ritual and burial traditions of the Iron Age communities. A life-size wooden figure, thought to be an idol, from a peat bog at Ballachulish, gives a rare glimpse of the ritual objects which would have been current in the Iron Age. The tradition of depositing metalwork in rivers and lochs continued throughout the Iron Age and wooden objects recovered from bogs may represent similar deposits. Deposits of animal bone are sometimes found under Iron Age buildings and these may represent offerings made when a house was built.

Several graves within the ditched area at **Cairnpapple,** West Lothian, are among the few burials which may date to the Iron Age. There is limited evidence that caves were used for burial and ritual practices at that time. At Sculptor's Cave, Moray, human bones dating to the Iron Age were recovered and their study demonstrated that the individuals had been beheaded, possibly for human sacrifice. There are also instances of human bone being deposited in disused buildings, for example at the settlement at the Howe in Orkney.

Hut circles

Hut circles dating to the Iron Age are found in all parts of Scotland, either on their own or in closed groups as at **New and Old Kinord**, Aboyne, or in unenclosed groups as at the **Ord** and **Kilphedir**, both in Sutherland. At Kilphedir a group of five huts was excavated and found to have a central hearth and a ring of posts which would have supported a conical roof. Hut circles are also found in and around the ramparts of many forts such as **Tap o' Noth**, Rhynie, where up to 150 hut platforms have been identified inside the fort.

Brochs

Brochs are a specialised form of Iron Age building, the majority found in the north and west of Scotland including the isles, with a few 'outliers' such as that at

Dun Troddan, Glenelg

Edin's Hall in Berwickshire. The brochs at **Mousa**, Shetland, **Dun Carloway**, Lewis, **Dun Dornaigil**, Sutherland and the Glenelg brochs, **Dun Telve** and **Dun Troddan**, are among the best examples in Scotland and display the 'classic' broch features. Broch towers were round drystone-built structures, their profile tapering slightly to the wallhead. They were constructed as a double wall held together with cross-slabs. The exterior was perforated by only one entrance – a narrow doorway leading through a passage to a central courtyard. Many passages have guard cells at one or both sides, and the door checks and bar holes for securing the main door are sometimes visible. Further entrances led off the courtyard to other cells, to stretches of gallery, or to stairs which wound up between the walls to upper floors. Voids are sometimes noted above the entrances, possibly to take the strain off the lintels. Scarcement ledges often run round the interior of the courtyard walls, presumably to hold the timbers for upper floors or the rafters for the roof.

Within the group of buildings classified as brochs there are many variations. It is unlikely that all brochs were broch towers and many were probably much lower than Mousa. There is also a major difference in structure between the northern and western brochs with the northern brochs being solid-based, that is, their galleries begin on the first floor, while the western brochs are 'ground-galleried'. Even within these two main groups there is much variation – **Dun Fiadhairt**, Skye, for example, has two entranceways.

Many of the northern brochs have settlements around them. While some of these buildings post-date the brochs, others would have been contemporary with their occupation. There are good excavated examples of such villages at **Clickhimin** and **Jarlshof**,

Clickhimmin

Shetland Mainland and **Gurness,** Orkney Mainland, as well as **Scatness,** Shetland which is currently under excavation. In the West the brochs are more likely to stand alone – **Dun Beag**, Skye, which is built on a rocky knoll, is one example.

Where brochs have been excavated, as at **Dun Mor, Vaul**, Tiree, the artefacts recovered – including querns, stone and metal tools, and pottery – suggest that these were the homes of farming families, even if presumably prosperous ones. However, the construction of the brochs, and in some cases their setting or additional external outworks, indicates a desire for defence. **Dun an Sticar**, North Uist, for example, was built on an island to make attack more difficult, and **Midhowe**, Rousay, and **Tirefour**, Lismore, have additional defences. In some cases a broch was built on the site of an earlier fort and perhaps made use of its defences – **Torwoodlee**, Galashiels, is one such example.

Other types of stone-built structure

In addition to brochs there is a multitude of substantial stone-built structures, including small duns, many of similar dimensions to brochs but without all the classic broch features, such as **Dun Ringill** and **Dun Ardtreck** on Skye, **Kildonan**, Kintyre, and **Castle Haven**, near Gatehouse of Fleet. Also of a similar size are wheelhouses which have radial stone piers dividing the area around the walls into cubicles. Wheelhouses have been found dug into the sand for extra shelter and also inserted into disused brochs as at **Jarlshof**, Shetland Mainland.

Crannogs

Crannogs are a settlement type found in many parts of Scotland, but particularly in central and southern areas. A crannog is an artificial island made of stone or timber – hundreds have been recorded around the shores of inland lochs in the Highlands and south-west, some of which date to the Iron Age. Many of these islands would have been built as a platform for a timber roundhouse. A crannog based on the excavated example of Oakbank, Loch Tay, has recently been reconstructed at the **Scottish Crannog Centre,** on Loch Tay at Kenmore. Where excavations have been carried out on crannogs, waterlogged material is often recovered, including leather, textiles and wooden artefacts which are seldom found on other sites.

Souterrains

Underground passages, known as souterrains, are another type of structure also dating to the Iron Age – some of the most complete like **Culsh**, Aboyne, still have their slabbed roof. Among the best examples are **Grain** and **Rennibister** on Orkney Mainland and **Castle Law,** near Edinburgh. The latter was built into a disused ditch, part of the rampart of an Iron Age fort.

Associated settlements have sometimes been found at excavated examples including **Ardestie** and **Carlungie**, Monifieth. At some of these settlements the souterrains were entered from the houses. Souterrains were probably used as storage cellars – some have chambers or cells within them.

Forts

While duns, brochs and larger roundhouses are certainly more substantial than would be necessary for a dwelling house and must have had a defensive or prestige aspect to their design, there are other stone-built structures for which a defensive function can be more strongly argued. At **Dun Gerashader**, Skye, for example, the natural defences of the site were incorporated into the design of the fort, with a stone rampart and several lines of upright stones, presumably to break up an attack, being added across the line of easiest access. Again at **Kemp's Walk**, Stranraer, a promontory was chosen and its neck was defended by a rampart.

Hilltops were a favoured location for forts. The most sizeable examples are in the south and east of Scotland and include **Eildon Hill** North, Melrose, which encloses over sixteen hectares. These hill forts are defended by strong ramparts. Some forts are enclosed by a single rampart but others have more than one phase of building. At **Arbory Hill**, Abington, a stone fort was built within earlier ditches and ramparts. The most elaborate ramparts have a framework of timbers. At **Finavon Fort**, Forfar, the timber-laced fort was destroyed by fire, the heat produced causing the stone and earth in the structure to fuse, or vitrify. The entrances to hill forts are often additionally protected by complex earthworks, and there is one example, **Dreva Craig**, Broughton, where the defences were strengthened by over a hundred stones set upright to break up an attack. In other cases the ramparts may have been for show as much as defence. **The Chesters**, East Lothian, is an example – here the fort is overlooked by higher ground.

Where excavation has been carried out it is often apparent that the hill forts were occupied over long periods. Excavations on the hill fort on **Traprain Law**, Haddington, for example, have recovered artefacts ranging in date from the Neolithic to the Early Historic period. Again at **Tynron Doon**, Dumfries and Galloway, occupation began in the Iron Age and ended with the construction of a tower house inside the enclosure, probably in the late 16th century. Many hill forts could have housed a sizeable community – around 300 hut circles have been identified within the fort on **Eildon Hill,** Melrose, and the traces of cultivation are often found on the adjacent slopes as at **Holyrood Park**, Edinburgh.

The Romans
The Roman army, under Gnaeus Julius Agricola, advanced into Scotland in AD 79, and Scotland entered history a year later with Tacitus' account of the advance. While Scotland was never truly 'Romanised' in the three hundred years or so during which there was a Roman presence in Scotland, the Romans left a legacy of defensive structures – camps and forts, and the Antonine Wall, begun around AD 142, which stretched from the Forth to the Clyde. A number of these sites are open to the public and listed in most guides to the period.

Cist, Temple Wood

a Wee Guide to
Prehistoric
Scotland

List of Prehistoric Sites

Map 1: Prehistoric Scotland

Map 1: Prehistoric Scotland

Orkney and Shetland see Map 2 page 34

ORKNEY

- Kirkwall

SHETLAND

- Lerwick

- Fraserburgh

Thurso
- Heritage Museum
- Cnoc Freiceadain
- Wick
- Achavanich
- Grey Cairns of Camster
- Hill o' Many Stanes
- Wag of Forse
- Kilphedir

- Dun Dornaigil

- The Ord

- Elgin

- Tap o' Noth
- Loanhead of Daviot
- Easter Aquorthies
- Archaeolink
- Sunhoney
- Aberdeen
- Cushnie
- Cullerlie
- Tomnaverie

- New and Old Kinord

- Ullapool

Museum and Art Gallery
- Inverness
- Clava Cairns
- Corrimony

- Clach an Trushal

LEWIS
- Dun Carloway / Doune Broch Centre
- Stornoway
- Museum nan Eilean
- Callanish

- Dun Fiadhairt
- Dun Gerashader
- Portree
- Dun Beag
- Dun Ardtreck
SKYE
- Dun Telve
- Dun Troddan
- Dun Ringill

- Rubh' an Dunain

NORTH UIST
- Unival
- Dun an Sticar
- Barpa Langass
- Pobull Fhinn

BARRA
- Dun Bharpa

A B C D E
1 2 3 4 5 6 7

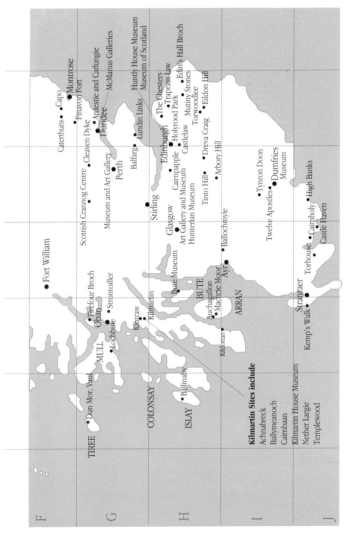

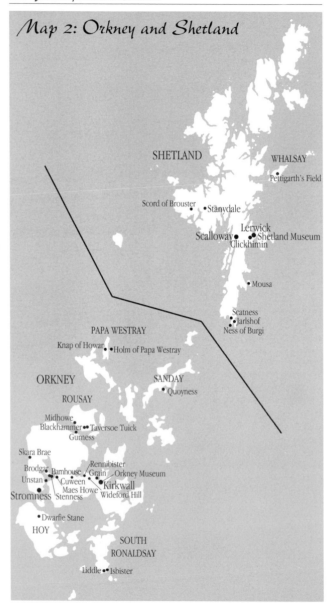

Map 2: Orkney and Shetland

SHETLAND

WHALSAY

• Pettigarth's Field

Scord of Brouster
•   • Stanydale

Lerwick
Scalloway •   •• Shetland Museum
Clickhimin

• Mousa

Scatness
• Jarlshof
Ness of Burgi

PAPA WESTRAY

Knap of Howar • •• Holm of Papa Westray

ORKNEY   SANDAY

ROUSAY   • Quoyness

Midhowe •
Blackhammer •• Taversoe Tuick
Gurness

Skara Brae

Brodgar Barnhouse Rennibister
Unstan • •• Grain   Orkney Museum
        • Cuween • Kirkwall
       Maes Howe
Stromness Stenness Wideford Hill

• Dwarfie Stane
HOY

SOUTH
RONALDSAY

Liddle •• Isbister

List of Prehistoric Sites and Museums

Achavanich Stone Setting

ND 187417   LR: 12   (Map ref: Map 1, C5)

Off A895, 6 miles N of Latheron, Achavanich, Caithness.

This is a horseshoe-shaped arrangement of 36 small standing stones – it is probable that there were originally 54 stones. The stones are short – the tallest is only 2 m high – and seem to have been set into a low mound. Some small slabs, possibly the remains of cists, protrude through the turf outside the north-east corner. Near the south-east is a round cairn, probably dating to the Neolithic period.

Achnabreck Cup and Ring Marks

HS   NR 856907   LR: 55   (Map ref: Map 1, G3)

1.5 miles NW of Lochgilphead, Kilmartin Glen, Argyll.

The cup-and-ring markings at Achnabreck are among the most impressive groups in Scotland. The site comprises two groups about 30 m apart. The lower

group consists of three areas, many with multi-ringed cups. The upper site has some of the largest ring-marks in Scotland, some almost 1 m in diameter, and includes double-ended spirals and a triple spiral. It is probable that the carvings were the work of several artists over a long period.

Access at all reasonable times.
Parking nearby – walk to site.
Tel: 0131 668 8800   Fax: 0131 668 8888

Arbory Hill Fort

NS 944238   LR: 72   (Map ref: Map 1, H5)
Off A74, 0.5 miles NE of Abington, Arbory Hill, Lanarkshire.

Three lines of defences representing two phases of fort building surround the summit of Arbory Hill. The earlier fort had two ditches and ramparts which were cut by five entrances. A circular stone-walled enclosure was later added. Hut circles can be traced inside the inner rampart and inside the stone enclosure.

Archaeolink

NJ 665257   LR: 38   (Map ref: Map 1, D6)
On B9002, Berryhill, Oyne, Aberdeenshire.

Exploring the mysteries of life 6000 years ago, the park features six indoor attractions, including an audio-visual presentation, interactive displays and recon-structions. In the park area is a reconstructed Iron Age farm, as well as a walk up to the site of a hill fort.

Open April-Oct, daily 10.00-17.00
Guided tours by arrangement. Audio-visual presentation. Gift shop. Restaurant. WC. Disabled

access. Car and coach parking. Group concessions. ££.
Tel: 01464 851500   Fax: 01464 851544
Web: www.archeolink.co.uk

Ardestie and Carlungie Souterrains

HS   NO 502344   LR: 54   (Map ref: Map G6)

Off B962, 1.25 miles N of Monifieth, Ardestie, Angus (signposted).

The souterrains at Ardestie and Carlungie are just over one mile apart. Both have been excavated and are displayed along with their associated stone buildings.

At Ardestie [NO 502344] there are the outlines of four huts one of which had an entrance into the souterrain. From the excavated artefacts the site was in use between AD 150 and AD 450. At Carlungie [NO 511359] there are the foundations of eight huts, seven of which are arranged around a paved courtyard. Four entrances led into the souterrain, one of which was off the courtyard.

Access at all reasonable times.
Parking nearby.
Tel: 0131 668 8800   Fax: 0131 668 8888

Auchagallon Cairn

HS   NR 893346   LR: 69   (Map ref: Map 1, H3)

Off A841, 4 miles N of Blackwaterfoot, Auchgallon, Arran (signposted).

The site at Auchagallon is an unusual monument with a stone cairn surrounded by a stone circle. The stone circle possibly formed the kerb of the cairn. The stones

are graded, with the tallest stones towards the sea, and there may also have been a deliberate distinction in the choice of stone. One stone on each side of the circle is grey granite, while the others are red sandstone. Excavation would be needed to resolve the many questions which this site poses.

Access at all reasonable times.
Parking nearby.
Tel: 0131 668 8800   Fax: 0131 668 8888

Balfarg Henge

NO 281031   LR: 59   (Map ref: Map 1, G6)
Off B969, 1 mile NE of Glenrothes, Balfarg, Fife.

The henge at Balfarg was excavated prior to the
construction of the surrounding housing estate. The
ditched area is 60 m across – the external bank did not
survive. Within the henge were various settings
including a timber circle built around 3000 BC (the
position of the posts are indicated by wooden markers)
and a stone circle of which two stones remain. The flat
slab in the centre of the henge is the capstone of one of
the later burials, which had a beaker in it. An archaeological trail leads past a setting of posts, representing
the position of the timbers in a ritual site used in the
fourth millennium BC, and the stone circle of Balbirnie
(moved from its original position after excavation).

Ballinaby Standing Stones

NR 219672   LR: 60   (Map ref: Map 1, H2)
Off B8018, 4.5 miles NW of Bruichladdich, Ballinaby, Islay.

Originally there was a group of three stones here – two
remain. The taller of the two, at almost 5 m high, is one
of the tallest standing stones in western Scotland. The
nearby stone, about 200 m to the north-east, is now
only 2 m high – it has been damaged.

Ballochmyle Cup and Ring Marks

NS 511255   LR: 70   (Map ref: Map 1, I4)
Off A76, 1 mile SE of Mauchline, Ballochmyle, Ayrshire.

The set of carvings at Ballochmyle, which were only

discovered in 1986, comprise a variety of motifs including cups, cup-and-rings and more geometric compositions. One of the largest groups of such markings in Britain, Ballochmyle is unusual in having been executed on a vertical face – horizontal faces were more often decorated in this way (eg **Achnabreck**, Argyll). The carvings are very fragile.

Ballymeanoch Standing Stones

NR 833965   LR: 62   (Map ref: Map 1, G3)

Off A816, 2 miles S of Kilmartin, Ballymeanoch, Kilmartin Glen, Argyll.

The stone settings at Ballymeanoch are part of the rich concentration of monuments in the Kilmartin Glen. There is an alignment of four stones and, parallel to this, two further stones and a fallen stone pierced with a hole close by. According to local custom, this stone was used in the sealing of contracts such as marriage

Dunchraigaig Cairn

vows where the two parties would join hands through the hole in the stone. The middle two stones in the alignment are marked with cup and rings, and one of the outer stones also has one cup carved on it.

Dunchraigaig Cairn [NR 833968] is nearby, as are Baluachraig Cup and Ring marks [NR 831969].

Access at all reasonable times.
Parking nearby.

Barnhouse Prehistoric Settlement

HY 306126   LR: 6   (Map ref: Map 2)
On A9055, 3.5 miles NE of Stromness, Barnhill, Orkney. A short walk along a signposted path from the Stones of Stenness car park.

The site at Barnhouse displays the reconstructed remains of a Neolithic village with houses very similar in design to those at **Skara Brae**. 'Grooved Ware' pottery recovered during the recent excavations indicates that Barnhouse was broadly contemporary with Skara Brae and also with the nearby **Stones of Stenness**. The excavations uncovered at least fifteen houses with the remains of box-beds, dressers and hearths, again like those found at Skara Brae. Unlike the Skara Brae houses, those at Barnhouse were not interconnected and they were free standing, not built into a midden. Two of the houses at Barnhouse were much bigger than the rest. One contained a hearth and a dresser but no beds and perhaps served as a meeting place.

Access at all reasonable times.
Explanatory boards. Parking.

Barpa Langass Chambered Cairn

NF 837657   LR: 18   (Map ref: Map 1, D1)

Off A867, 5 miles W of Lochmaddy, Ben Langass, North Uist.

Barpa Langass is a great round cairn of stones, 25 m in diameter and over 4 m high. The kerb of boulders which surrounded the cairn can still be seen, as can the

outline of the forecourt, funnelling in to the entrance. The entrance passage and the oval chamber are roofed with large slabs and the walls also include some substantial stones. Entry into the chamber is now difficult and may be dangerous. It would never have been possible to fit many people into the chamber and the forecourt may have been the focus for ritual.

Access at all reasonable times.
Parking.

Blackhammer Chambered Cairn

HS   HY 414276   LR: 6   (Map ref: Map 2)

On B9065, S of Island of Rousay, Orkney.

This chambered tomb has been excavated and is now entered down a ladder through a modern concrete roof. The original entrance opened from the middle of the cairn. The chamber has seven burial compartments. The slabs on the exterior of the cairn were arranged in a triangular pattern some of which is visible near the entrance.

Access at all reasonable times.
Tel: 0131 668 8800   Fax: 0131 668 8888

Cairnholy Chambered Cairns

HS   NX 518540   LR: 83   (Map ref: Map 1, J4)

Off A75, 6.5 miles SE of Creetown, Dumfries and Galloway (signposted).

Overlooking Wigtown Bay are the remains of two chambered tombs. The larger stones of the passage

and chamber are now the most prominent feature of the monuments, most of the cairn material having been removed. Clyde cairns have a trapezoidal outline and the entrance is situated in the wider end, often at the centre of a forecourt with a facade of upright stones. Cairnholy I differs slightly from the classic plan having straight sides. Its forecourt is lined with narrow stones. On excavation traces of fires and pottery sherds were found in the forecourt and it is probable that this area was a focus for ceremonies connected with the burials. Cairnholy II is the smaller of the two cairns. No traces of a facade were found during excavation.

Access at all reasonable times.
Car parking.
Tel: 0131 668 8800   Fax: 0131 668 8888

Cairnbaan Cup and Ring Marks

HS   NR 838910   LR: 55   (Map ref: Map 1, G3)
On A841, 2.5 miles NW of Lochgilphead, near Cairnbaan Hotel, Argyll (signposted).

At this site there are two outcrops decorated with cups and cups and rings, some having grooves across the rings.

Access at all reasonable times.
Parking nearby.
Tel: 0131 668 8800   Fax: 0131 668 8888

Cairnpapple Ceremonial Site

HS   NS 987717   LR: 65   (Map ref: Map 1, H5)
Off B792, 3 miles N of Bathgate, West Lothian (signposted).

Cairnpapple was a ceremonial site for some 1500 years from at least 2800 BC. It may have been chosen as a ritual focus because of the spectacular views from the summit – from the Bass Rock in the east to Arran in the west, the Pentlands and Moorfoot Hills to the south and the Ochil Hills to the north. The earliest burials were in an arc of pits. In the centre of the arc were three standing stones. Around 2500 BC this was surrounded by a henge within which was a circle of 24 timber posts or standing stones. A burial with 'Beaker' pottery was inserted within the circle and marked with a standing stone. Later a burial in a large cist was added beside the Beaker burial, and a large cairn erected over them (this is now reflected by the modern concrete dome). The cairn was later enlarged and a boulder kerb added. The site continued to be used for burials until at least the Iron Age.

Open Apr-Sep, daily 9.00-18.30.
Explanatory display. Short walk to monument. Car parking. Group concessions. £.
Tel: 01506 634622   Fax: 0131 668 8888

Callanish Standing Stones

HS   NB 213330   LR: 8   (Map ref: Map 1, C2)
Off A858, 14 miles W of Stornoway, Callanish, Lewis (signposted).

The main stone setting at the famous Callanish complex is a circle of thirteen tall grey stones with a double row of stones leading from it to the north, and single rows leading to the west, south and east. A tall stone, 4.7 m high stands within the circle beside a small chambered tomb. From radiocarbon-dated material this tomb was built a few generations later than the circle. It has been suggested that the setting was designed as a lunar observatory. A number of smaller

settings dot the area around Callanish. There is a Historic Scotland visitor centre.

Sites open all year; visitor centre open Apr-Oct, Mon-Sat 10.00-19.00; Oct-Mar, Mon-Sat 10.00-16.00.
Visitor Centre: Explanatory displays. Gift shop. Tearoom. WC. Disabled access. Car and coach parking.
Tel: 01851 621422   Fax: 01851 621446
Email: calanais.centre@btinternet.com

Capo Long Barrow

NO 633644   LR: 45   (Map ref: Map 1, F6)

Off A92, 4 miles NE of Brechin, Capo, Kincardine and Deeside. Follow the signposted path.

Capo is a Neolithic earthen long mound 80 m long and 28 m wide at the east end. From excavated examples the wider eastern end would be expected to cover burials and timber mortuary structures. While stone-built tombs are more common in Scotland, there are many examples of mounds of earth and turf in the south and east. The mound is situated in a clearing in Inglismaldie forest, on a natural terrace above the River Esk.

Castle Haven

NX 594483   LR: 83   (Map ref: Map 1, J4)

Off B727, 2 miles E of Borgue, Kirkandrews, Dumfries and Galloway. Follow the path to the shore.

This is a D-shaped galleried dun with the straight part of the wall along the cliff edge. The dun has two

entrances, a main entrance at the north and a smaller one leading to the shore. Six entrances lead off the central courtyard into the galleries. It is not certain if the surrounding wall was contemporary with the dun. Earlier this century the dun was cleared out and restored by the landowner.

Castlelaw Hill Fort

HS   NT 229638   LR: 66   (Map ref: Map 1, H6)

Off A702, near Glencorse, Castlelaw, Midlothian (signposted).

Excavations at Castlelaw in the 1930s and 1940s revealed that prior to the fort defined by the multiple

ramparts there was a palisaded enclosure dating to the first millennium BC and a fort with a single rampart. A 20 m long souterrain was built into one of the ditches once the defences were no longer being maintained. Midway along the passage is a corbelled cell.

Access at all reasonable times.
Car and coach parking.
Tel: 0131 668 8800   Fax: 0131 668 8888

Caterthuns Forts

HS   NO 555668   LR: 44   (Map ref: Map 1, F6)

Off A94, near Menmuir, 5 miles NW of Brechin, Angus.

The forts of Brown Caterthun and White Caterthun sit atop neighbouring hills just over 1.5 miles apart. The Brown Caterthun [NO 555668] has heather-covered boulders, whereas the White Caterthun has ramparts of light-coloured stones. The higher of the two is the White Caterthun [NO 547660] which has a double rampart. The Brown Caterthun has several ramparts around the summit and, further down the hill, a wall (cut by nine entrances) surrounded by a double rampart. Still further down slope are two more ramparts with an external ditch. Recent excavations at the Brown Caterthun indicate a date of around 700 BC for the inner rampart, and 500-300 BC for the middle group.

Access at all reasonable times.
Parking nearby
Tel: 0131 668 8800   Fax: 0131 668 8888

Chesters Hill Fort

HS   NT 507782   LR: 66   (Map ref: Map 1, H6)

Off B1377, 1 mile S of Drem, The Chesters, East Lothian.

The Chesters is an oval fort with complex ramparts. Its position in the landscape is unusual as it occupies a low ridge, overlooked by a rocky scarp, not a naturally easily-defended situation. Within the hill fort are over twenty hut-circle platforms. From its situation the site was built for show as much as for defence.

Access at all reasonable times – visit involves walk.
Parking nearby.
Tel: 0131 668 8800   Fax: 0131 668 8888

Clach an Trushal Standing Stone

NB 375538   LR: 8   (Map ref: Map 1, B2)

Off A857, 2.5 miles N of Barvas, Ballantrushal, Lewis.

This standing stone is around 6 m in height, one of the tallest in Scotland.

Clava Cairns (Balnuaran of Clava)

NTS   NH 757445   LR: 27   (Map ref: Map 1, D5)

Off B9006 or B851, 6 miles E of Inverness, Highlands (signposted).

This site gives its name to a distinctive type of cairn with a central chamber and a kerb of large boulders. A circle of standing stones surrounds the cairn. At Clava there is a line of three cairns. The central one is a Clava ring cairn which has no passage to the chamber, while the other two are Clava passage graves. Most Clava cairns are found around Inverness and the Black Isle and the Spey Valley. Both cremations and inhumations

have been uncovered during excavations of these type of cairns. The Clava cairns seem to have been the burial places of a few individuals rather than collective tombs for whole communities. Cup marked stones were found built into each of the passage graves. Recent excavations at the site indicate that the Clava cairns are a fairly late form of chambered tomb, being built from around 2000 BC.

Access at all reasonable times.
Parking.
Tel: 0131 668 8800   Fax: 0131 668 8888

Cleaven Dyke

NO 165405   LR: 53   (Map ref: Map 1, G5)
On A93, 3 miles SW of Blairgowrie, Meikleour, Perthshire.

The Cleaven Dyke is a 2.3 km long bank flanked by ditches, thought to mark out a route along which participants in communal ceremonies would have passed. An oval mound at the north-west end is thought to be the earliest part of the monument to which segments were added, possibly over many years. Similar cursus (earth banks believed to have been used for ritual or funerary purposes) have been recognised in other parts of Scotland.

Clickhimin Broch

HS   HU 464408   LR: 4   (Map ref: Map 2)
Off A970, 1 mile SW of Lerwick, Clickhimin, Shetland (signposted).

The settlement at Clickhimin was originally on an island joined to the shore by a causeway. The first settlement was in the mid-first millennium BC. A small

oval house of this period survives to the north-west of the broch. Towards the end of the millennium the islet was surrounded by a stone wall and the massive blockhouse built at the entrance to the enclosure. The blockhouse, which survives to a height of over 5 m, would have had to have been passed through to reach the broch tower constructed in the centre of the islet. When the broch went out of use, a roundhouse was built inside it. At the end of the causeway, set into the path, is a stone with two footprints carved into it. Where similar stones have been found elsewhere they have been linked with inauguration rites of kings in the Early Historic period.

Access at all reasonable times.
Parking nearby.
Tel: 0131 668 8800   Fax: 0131 668 8888

Cnoc Freiceadain Chambered Cairns

HS   ND 012653   LR: 12   (Map ref: Map 1, B5)
Off A836, 6 miles SW of Thurso, Cnoc Freiceadain, Caithness. Reached by a signposted path.

The cairns on Cnoc Freiceadain are two long cairns, now grass-covered. The largest is the southern cairn which at 78 m is one of Scotland's largest. One cairn has horns at one end, the other has horns at both ends. A number of round mounds were probably incorporated under the long cairns as at **Grey Cairns of Camster**.

Access at all reasonable times.
Tel: 0131 668 8800   Fax: 0131 668 8888

Corrimony Chambered Cairn

HS   NH 383303   LR: 26   (Map ref: Map 1, D4)

Off A831, 8.5 miles W of Drumnadrochit, Glen Urquhart, Highlands (signposted).

Corrimony is a Clava cairn (see **Clava Cairns**), having a circular cairn with a kerb retaining the cairn material, and a central circular chamber reached by a passage. Surrounding the cairn is a ring of eleven standing stones. A large cup-marked stone lying on top of the cairn may have capped the chamber. Soil stains noted during excavations in the 1950s indicate that the chamber contained a crouched body.

Access at all reasonable times.
Parking nearby.
Tel: 0131 668 8800   Fax: 0131 668 8888

Cullerlie Stone Circle

HS   NJ 786042   LR: 38   (Map ref: Map 1, E6)

Off B9215, 3 miles SW of Westhill, Cullerlie, Aberdeenshire.

The stone circle at Cullerlie comprises eight unshaped boulders. Inside the circle are eight small kerbed cairns, a central one with a double kerb, the other seven with single kerbs. When the site was excavated,

only one of the outer cairns was found to be undisturbed. Under the cairn stones there was a capstone covering a circular pit which contained cremated human bone and charcoal.

Access at all reasonable times.
Parking.
Tel: 0131 668 8800   Fax: 0131 668 8888

Culsh Souterrain

HS   NJ 504054   LR: 37   (Map ref: Map 1, E6)
On B9119, 1 mile E of Tarland, Culsh, Aberdeenshire.

This is a well-preserved souterrain, a curving passage about 12 m long and almost 2 m wide and high. The roof, which comprises large slabs, is intact. There has been no excavation to determine whether there were associated buildings above ground.

Access at all reasonable times.
Tel: 0131 668 8800   Fax: 0131 668 8888

Cuween Hill Chambered Cairn

HS   HY 364128   LR: 6   (Map ref: Map 2)

Off A965, 7 miles NW of Kirkwall, 0.5 miles S of Finstown, Orkney (signposted).

The chambered tomb at Cuween is notable for having contained the skulls of 24 dogs, found on the floor of the chamber during excavations at the beginning of the century. It is possible that the dogs were a totem of the group using the tomb. Skeletal remains from at least eight humans were also found. The tomb has a rectangular main chamber with a cell leading off each side. One of the cells is divided into two. The walls were very well built, using thin flagstones. The roof is modern.

Access at all reasonable times – a torch will be needed and the key should be collected from the farm.
Parking.
Tel: 0131 668 8800   Fax: 0131 668 8888

Doune Broch Centre

NB 190412   LR: 8   (Map ref: Map 1, C2)

Off A858, 14 miles NW of Stornoway, Carloway, Lewis.

The centre features an interpretative chamber called 'Scenes from the Broch' and a graphics display, which recreates views of nearby **Dun Carloway Broch** (see separate entry) – when complete – and illustrates the life of the inhabitants.

Open Apr-Oct, Mon-Sat 10.00-18.00.
Explanatory displays. Gift shop. WC. Car and coach parking.
Tel: 01851 643338/01851 621422   Fax: 01851 621446
Email: calanais.centre@btinternet.com

Dreva Craig Fort

NT 126353   LR: 72   (Map ref: Map 1, H5)

Off A701, 5.5 miles E of Biggar, Dreva Craig, Borders.

On the way along Dreva Craig to the fort a number of hut-circles and field systems, probably dating to the late Iron Age, are visible. Some are later than the fort as they are built into the rubble of the walls. There are further round houses inside the fort. The fort has two stone ramparts with the entrance to the east. Down the slope to the south of the fort the defences were strengthened by a defensive outwork, over 100 stones set upright on the hillside to break up an attack.

Dun Ardtreck

NG 335358   LR: 32   (Map ref: Map 1, D2)

Off B8009, 3.5 miles NW of Corbost, Portnalong, Ardtreck Point, Skye.

This site was termed a semi-broch by its excavator and it is in effect about two-thirds of a broch, with the final section of defence being provided by the 20 m high cliff on which it stands. The entrance has door checks and a guard cell, and two entrances lead from the interior to stretches of gallery. Finds from the excavations included the door handle – an iron ring – fused to the stones on the passage floor during a fire.

Dun Beag Broch

HS   NG 339386   LR: 32   (Map ref: Map 1, D2)

On A863, 8 miles S of Dunvegan, Struanmore, Skye (signposted).

Dun Beag is one of Skye's best preserved brochs. From

its perch on a rocky knoll it commands fine views of
Loch Bracadale and the Cuillin Hills. The broch was
excavated in the early part of the century. Along the
paved entrance passage the door checks and bar-holes
are visible. Entrances led off the central court to a cell,
to a stretch of gallery (this entrance is now blocked)
and to a staircase winding up between the walls. A
range of artefacts was recovered during the excavations including pottery, stone whorls and scrapers, and
more personal items such as beads, rings and pins.

Access at all reasonable times.
Parking.

Dun Bharpa Chambered Cairn

NF 671019   LR: 31   (Map ref: Map 1, E1)
Off A888, 2.5 miles N of Castlebay, Craigston, Barra.

Although it is not possible to enter this chambered
cairn, it is impressive for its size – around 5 m high
and 25 m in diameter. Some of the slabs of the kerb are
visible as is the cover slab of the chamber.

Dun Carloway Broch

HS   NB 190412   LR: 8   (Map ref: Map 1, C2)
Off A858, 15 miles NW of Stornoway, Carloway, Lewis.

Dun Carloway is the best preserved broch in the
Western Isles, its tallest portion standing to 9 m. There
is a guard cell off the entrance passage. Inside the
courtyard are three doorways leading to the staircase
opposite the main entrance and to side cells. The
natural rock protrudes jaggedly into the interior of the

courtyard and, given this, it would seem likely that
there was a timber floor erected higher up which
provided the main living space. A ledge of stones, or
scarcement, protruding from the wall, could have
supported such a floor. There is a small visitors centre,
the **Doune Broch Centre**, at the site.

Access at all reasonable times.
Car and coach parking. The Doune Broch Centre is
nearby.
Tel: 0131 668 8800   Fax: 0131 668 8888

Dun Dornaigil Broch

HS   NC 457450   LR: 9   (Map ref: Map 1, C4)

Off A838, 3.5 miles S of end of Loch Hope, Dun Dornaigil, Caithness.

Dun Dornaigil (Dun Dornadilla) survives to almost 7 m in one section (now supported by a modern buttress) which places it among the best preserved examples in Scotland. The entrance is crowned with a huge triangular lintel. The broch has not been excavated and the interior is full of rubble.

Access at all reasonable times.
Parking.
Tel: 0131 668 8800   Fax: 0131 668 8888

Dun Fiadhairt Broch

NG 231504   LR: 23   (Map ref: OO)

Off A850, 2.5 miles NW of Dunvegan, Fiadhairt, Skye.

Dun Fiadhairt (Dun an Iardhard) is unusual in having two entrances. As well as the main entrance, a second entrance leads into a gallery and then out through the external wall. Three further doorways from the interior lead to two cells within the wall, and to a gallery with a flight of stairs. The broch was excavated in the early part of the century, and finds included an unusual amber necklace which had been hidden in a recess in the wall.

Dun Gerashader Fort

NG 489452   LR: 23   (Map ref: Map 1, D2)

On A865, 0.5 miles N of Portree, Dun Gerashader, Skye.

The builders of Dun Gerashader made full use of the

natural defences of the site when designing their fort, which occupies the top of a rocky eminence with only one direction of easy access. This approach has been crossed by a 4 m thick rampart. Lines of huge boulders placed across the slope in front of the rampart would have slowed down an attack.

Dun Mor Broch, Vaul

NM 042492   LR: 46   (Map ref: Map 1, G2)
Off B8069, 2.5 miles N of Scarinish, Vaul, Tiree.

This broch, excavated in the 1970s, occupies a rocky knoll circled by a stone wall. The entrance passage has a corbelled guard cell and door checks and also a pivot stone for the door. The broch, which survives up to 2 m high, is of ground galleried form. Several doors led into the gallery and one, almost opposite the main entrance, led to the stairway. Radiocarbon dates for material recovered during the excavations, as well as a long sequence of pottery, indicate that the broch was constructed in the first century BC but that it contin-ued to be used until the Norse period.

Dun Ringill

NG 562171   LR: 32   (Map ref: Map 1, E3)
Off A881, 11 miles SW of Broadford, Kilmarie, Skye.

Dun Ringill is a galleried dun – a cell, gallery and entrance can still be seen although the entrance has undergone some alterations. Inside the dun are the foundations of two medieval rectangular buildings. The dun had a strong wall and ditch strengthening the defences on the landward side.

Dun Telve Broch

HS   NG 829172   LR: 33   (Map ref: Map 1, E3)
Off A87, 2 miles SE of Glenelg, Gleann Beag, Lochalsh.

The Glenelg brochs, Dun Telve and **Dun Troddan** are two of the best preserved brochs in Scotland. A large

part of the wall of Dun Telve is missing but within the remaining sector of the wall are scarcements to support upper floors, and voids above the interior doors. The entrance has a bar-hole and door checks. There are various outbuildings around the broch although they may be later in date. Artefacts recov-

Dun Troddan – see next page

ered when the site was excavated included pottery fragments, stone cups (possibly used as lamps) and a few quern stones.

Access at all reasonable times.
Parking nearby.
Tel: 0131 668 8800   Fax: 0131 668 8888

Dun Troddan Broch

HS NG 833172 LR: 33 (Map ref: Map 1, E3)
Off A87, 2.5 miles SE of Glenelg, Corrary, Gleann Beag, Lochalsh.

Dun Troddan is the neighbour of **Dun Telve**, located less than 0.5 miles further along the glen. As with Dun Telve a sector of the wall survives and the structure of the building – two skins held together with horizontal slabs – can be seen. It is possible to go up a section of the staircase within the gallery. Off the entrance is a corbelled guard cell. When the site was excavated in 1920 a circle of posts was located in the central area, presumably to hold the posts which supported an upper timber floor.

Access at all reasonable times.
Parking nearby.
Tel: 0131 668 8800   Fax: 0131 668 8888

Dun an Sticar Broch

NF 898778 LR: 18 (Map ref: Map 1, D2)
On B893, 6 miles N of Lochmaddy, North Uist.

Dun an Sticar survives to a height of more than 3 m

making it one of the best preserved brochs in the Western Isles. A rectangular house inside is probably medieval in date. The causeway linking the island with the neighbouring one is probably also medieval in date, and two causeways link this island to the mainland.

View from exterior – care should be taken.
Parking nearby.

Dwarfie Stane Rock Cut Tomb

HS   HY 244005   LR: 7   (Map ref: Map 2)
Off B9047, N end of island of Hoy, off the road to Rackwick, Orkney.

Named 'Dvergasteinn' by the Norse settlers who thought it to have been the home of dwarfs, the Dwarfie Stane is, from its plan, most likely to be a Neolithic tomb. Hollowed out of the stone are a pair of rounded cells, one on each side of a passage, and divided from the passage by a kerb. The cell on the right has a low step or pillow within it. A number of

graffiti inscriptions are testament to early visitors to the site and include some lines in Persian by Major W Mounsey, a British spy in Persia, which date to 1850.

Access at all reasonable times.
Tel: 0131 668 8800   Fax: 0131 668 8888

Easter Aquorthies Stone Circle

HS   NJ 244005   LR: 7   (Map ref: Map 1, D6)

Off A96, 3 miles W of Inverurie, Easter Aquorthies, Aberdeenshire.

The circle, almost 20 m in diameter, has nine stones graded in height and set in a bank, as well as a recumbent and two flankers. There are a further two stones in front of the recumbent, perhaps delineating a ceremonial area. The stones in the circle are all pink porphyry, except that beside the east flanker which is red jasper; the flankers are grey granite; and the recumbent is red granite. This deliberate use of different types of stone is may be significant. The raised area

in the centre of the circle indicates the presence of a burial cairn.

Access at all reasonable times.
Parking nearby.
Tel: 0131 668 8800   Fax: 0131 668 8888

Edin's Hall Broch

HS   NT 772603   LR: 38   (Map ref: Map 1, H6)
Off A6112, 2.5 miles N of Preston, Borders (signposted).

The site at Edin's Hall comprises an oval fort with double rampart and ditches and a broch. The fort is probably the earlier of the two. The broch was built in a corner of the fort. Compared to the northern brochs it is very large, having an internal diameter of 17 m and walls up to 5 m thick. Within the walls are various cells including guard cells off the entrance passage. The hut circles in the interior are probably of various dates – some would have been contemporary with the fort, others overlie the defences.

Access at all reasonable times – 1.5 miles walk.
Parking nearby.

Eildon Hill Fort

NT 555238   LR: 73   (Map ref: Map 1, H6)

Off A6091, 1 mile SE of Melrose, Eildon, Borders (footpath).

The summit of Eildon Hill North, the largest of three peaks above Melrose and the Tweed, has been occupied since at least the Bronze Age. Some of the 300 or so houses (represented by house-platforms) date to the

late Bronze Age but others will be of Iron Age date. On the west end of the summit are traces of a Roman signal station which was set within a circular enclosure. The hill can be seen for more than 20 miles in most directions.

Finavon Fort

NO 506556   LR: 54   (Map ref: Map 1, F6)

Off B9134, 4 miles NE of Forfar, Hill of Finavon, Angus.

The ramparts of the fort on Hill of Finavon are massive, over 6 m thick, and straight rather than following the contours of the hilltop. The fort was destroyed by fire – the heat was so intense that the core of the rampart vitrified. In the interior of the fort to the east is a rock-cut tank.

Grain Souterrain

HS   HY 441116   LR: 6   (Map ref: Map 2)
Off A965, 0.5 miles NW of Kirkwall, industrial estate, Orkney.

The earth-house at Grain is almost 2 m below ground surface and very well preserved. A flight of steps led down to a curving, sloping passage, roofed by slabs, by which entry was gained to the kidney-shaped chamber. The chamber roof, also formed by slabs, was supported by four stone pillars, their height extended by the use of 'eke' stones where they were not tall enough. Excavations at ground level above the chamber uncovered a hearth, animal bones and shells indicating that the earth-house had been part of a larger settlement.

Access at all reasonable times.
Tel: 0131 668 8800   Fax: 0131 668 8888

Grey Cairns of Camster

HS   ND 260442   LR: 12   (Map ref: Map 1, C5)
Off A9, 5 miles N of Lybster, Camster, Watten, Caithness (signposted).

The massive cairns at Camster, only 200 m apart, stand out from their bleak moorland surroundings. Camster Round Cairn is at least 18 m in diameter. The entrance to the chamber is set midway along a straight facade. Entry to an antechamber is marked by a couple of portal stones and a further pair of stones mark the entry to the chamber. Human bones, pottery and flint were found during the nineteenth century excavations – similar finds were made in the long cairn. The tomb was completely filled with earth and stones after its final use. The long cairn is 70 m long and completely covered two other separate round cairns. One of these round cairns has a simple chamber, while the other has a passage, antechamber, main chamber and side cell. Short 'horns' form forecourts at each end of the long cairn.

Access at all reasonable times.
Parking.
Tel: 0131 668 8800   Fax: 0131 668 8888

Gurness Broch

HS   HY 381268   LR: 6   (Map ref: Map 2)
Off A966, 1 mile NE of Evie, Gurness, Orkney (signposted).

Excavated in the 1930s, Gurness is a good example of a broch and its surrounding settlement. The settlement consists of a number of buildings between the broch and its ramparts and ditches. Some of the houses date

to the later Iron Age when distinctive house forms were built. One, with five cells and a hearth, has been reconstructed beside the visitors centre. The broch itself has a solid wall base with a guard cell on each side of the entrance passage. In the courtyard are various structures, some of which date to the secondary occupation, including a well which is reached down some stone steps.

Open Apr-Sep, daily 9.30-18.30; last ticket 30 mins before closing – combined ticket available for Orkney monuments.
Explanatory displays. Disabled access. Car and limited coach parking. Group concessions. £.
Tel/Fax: 01856 751414

High Banks Cup and Ring Marks

NX 709489   LR: 84   (Map ref: Map 1, J5)
Off A711, 2 miles SE of Kirkcudbright, SE of High Banks farm, Dumfries and Galloway.

The site at High Banks has some of south-west Scotland's most impressive cup-and-ring carvings. At the south of the greywacke outcrop are over 350 cup marks, some grouped together to form designs, and many examples of cup-and-rings, some with multiple rings.

Hill o' Many Stanes (Stone Setting)

HS   ND 295384   LR: 11   (Map ref: Map 1, C5)
Off A9, 4 miles NE of Lybster, Mid Clyth, Caithness (signposted).

This stone setting, also known as the Mid Clyth stone rows, is a fan-shaped arrangement of over 200 standing stones set in 22 rows down the side of the hill. It is estimated that if the rows were complete the arrangement would originally have comprised over 600 stones. The function of the site is not known but it may have been an astronomical observatory.

Access at all reasonable times.
Tel: 0131 668 8800   Fax: 0131 668 8888

Holm of Papa Westray Chambered Cairns

HS   HY 509518   LR: 5   (Map ref: Map 2)
Island and Holm of Papa Westray, Orkney (one at each end of the island).

There are two chambered tombs on the Holm of Papa Westray. The one at the north of the island has a chamber divided into four by upright slabs and there is a cell off the end compartment. The latter was part of an earlier tomb. At the south of the island is another tomb, with twelve side cells, including two double cells. Entry to the chamber is down a ladder through the modern concrete roof.

Access at all reasonable times.
Tel: 0131 668 8800   Fax: 0131 668 8888

Holyrood Park Prehistoric Settlements

NT 274734   LR: 66   (Map ref: Map 1, H6)
Off A1, 1 mile E of Edinburgh Castle, Holyrood Park, Edinburgh.

The hills of Holyrood Park bear evidence for fortifications, settlements and ancient farming. On the high eminence of Arthur's Seat is a large fort enclosed by two stone ramparts. Above Samson's Ribs and on the hillside by Dunsapie Loch are two more forts. Hut circle remains include a number on the hillside east of Hunter's Bog. In the absence of excavation it is very difficult to date these sites but they probably date from the late Bronze Age and Iron Age.

Access at all reasonable times.
Parking.

Isbister Chambered Cairn (Tomb of the Eagles)

ND 470845   LR: 7   (Map ref: Map 2)

Off B9041, 5 miles S of St Margaret's Hope, SE side of South Ronaldsay, Orkney (signposted).

The tomb at Isbister was excavated in the 1970s and a stalled cairn was uncovered, the main chamber being divided into three by stone slabs. At each end is a partitioned area, originally shelved. The roof is modern – the original roof appears to have been removed when the tomb went out of use so that the chamber could be filled with earth and stones. Three side cells lead off the chamber. The remains of about 340 people were recovered during the excavations as well as bones and talons from white-tailed sea eagles, giving the tomb its more popular name, the 'Tomb of the Eagles'. At Liddle Farm is a display about the excavations, and the **Liddle** burnt mound can also be visited from here.

Open Apr-Oct daily 10.00-20.00, Nov-Mar 10.00-12.00 or by arrangement.
Exhibition and guided tours. WC. Disabled access. Car and coach parking. Group concessions. £.
Tel: 01856 831339

Jarlshof Broch and Settlement

HS   HU 398095   LR: 4   (Map ref: Map 2)

Off A970, Sumburgh Head, 22 miles S of Lerwick, Shetland (signposted).

The earliest buildings at Jarlshof date to the Neolithic period – traces of oval houses can be seen near the visitor centre. There is evidence that one of the

Neolithic houses was used for metalworking during the Bronze Age. Iron Age buildings include several roundhouses, a broch and three wheelhouses (circular buildings with radial stone piers forming alcoves around a central hearth). Occupation continued after the Iron Age with the construction of some cellular late Iron Age houses, through the Norse period when some rectangular structures were constructed, and into the 17th century when the Laird's house was built. There is a small visitor centre with artefacts from excavations.

Open Apr-Sep, daily 9.30-6.30
Visitor centre with exhibition. Gift shop. Car and coach parking. Group concessions. £.
Tel/Fax: 01950 460112

Kemp's Walk Fort

NW 975598   LR: 82   (Map ref: Map 1, J3)

Off B738, 4.5 miles W of Stranraer, Larbrax, Dumfries and Galloway.

Kemp's Walk is a promontory fort overlooking Broadsea Bay. It has three large ramparts and ditches crossing the northern approach. The other sides of the promontory have steeper slopes and would have been easier to defend. There are no traces of hut circles within the fort. This is the largest of Galloway's promontory forts, measuring 83 m by 44 m.

Kildonan Dun

NR 780227   LR: 68   (Map ref: Map 1, I3)

On B842, 5 miles NE of Campbeltown, Kildonan, Kintyre.

Excavations at this drystone-walled, D-shaped dun indicate that it was built in the first or second century AD and then reoccupied later in the ninth to twelfth centuries. The wall is 2 m thick and the door check and bar holes can still be seen, as can the double stairway to the wall-head and a mural cell. The dun was occupied into medieval times.

Kilmartin House Museum

NR 834989   LR: 55   (Map ref: Map 1, G3)

On A816, 9 miles N of Lochgilphead, Kilmartin, Argyll.

The Kilmartin House Museum features an archaeological interpretation of the many prehistoric monuments found in Kilmartin Glen. The fine museum features artefacts and reconstructions, and there is an impressive audio-visual presentation.

Open all year, daily 10.00-17.30.
Guided tours by arrangement. Audio-visual and explanatory displays. Gift and book shop. Cafe. WC. Disabled access and WC. Car parking. Group concessions. ££.
Tel: 01546 510278   Fax: 01546 510330
Web: www.kht.org.uk

Kilphedir Broch and Hut Circles

NC 995189   LR: 17   (Map ref: Map 1, C5)
Off A897, Kilphedir, Sutherland.

The broch, which is rubble-filled, is situated on a hilltop, surrounded by a series of ramparts and ditches. Down slope from the broch are a number of hut-circles including a group of five which have been excavated. Evidence for hearths were found during the excavations and a ring of post holes was uncovered inside one of the huts. The posts may have supported the rafters of a conical roof. Pottery, stone and flint tools and quern stones were recovered. From the dating evidence, some of the huts may have been contemporary with the broch.

Kintraw Cairns and Standing Stone

NM 830050   LR: 55   (Map ref: Map 1, G3)
On A816, 4 miles N of Kilmartin, Kintraw, Argyll.

The site at Kintraw has three elements – a large cairn, a small cairn and a standing stone. The cairns were excavated between 1956 and 1960. The larger of the cairns was surrounded by a kerb and was found to have a slab-built box or cist adjoining the kerb. As at **Strontoiller**, a large amount of quartz was found, this time around the kerb. Some cremated bone was recovered as well as shells, animal bones and six jet beads. The site has been interpreted as marking the sunset at the mid-winter solstice as the sun set through a notch in the Paps of Jura, 27 miles away.

Knap of Howar Prehistoric Settlement

HS   HY 483519   LR: 5   (Map ref: Map 2)
Island of Papa Westray, Orkney (signposted track).

Excavations in the 1930s and 1970s revealed two rectilinear stone-built structures, connected by a doorway. Traces of posts indicated timber roofing. The entrance to the larger building led into a room with a bench along one wall. Stone slabs partition off a smaller room which, from its hearth and quern may have been used for the preparation and cooking of food. The smaller building is divided into three, again by stone slabs. Recesses built into the wall of one of the rooms indicates that it was a store. Bone and stone implements and a quantity of pottery were recovered during the excavations.

Access at all reasonable times.
Tel: 0131 668 8800   Fax: 0131 668 8888

Liddle Burnt Mound

ND 464841   LR: 7   (Map ref: Map 2)
Off B9041, 4 miles S of St Margaret's Hope, Liddle, Orkney (signposted).

Over 400 burnt mounds are known in Orkney and Shetland and where any dating evidence has been recovered during excavation they seem to be Bronze Age in date. Liddle Burnt Mound is one of very few to have been excavated. Before excavation the site comprised a 2 m high mound of burnt stones. Excavation revealed a central stone-built trough surrounded by paving and a stone wall, possibly a windbreak. A hearth was set in an alcove. The theory is that stones were heated in the fire and dropped into water in the trough, heating the water to boiling when food was then added for cooking. The heat would have been maintained by adding more stones until cooking was complete. It has also been suggested that the burnt mounds really served as saunas, although the cooking option is currently favoured.

Loanhead of Daviot Stone Circle

HS   NJ 747288   LR: 38   (Map ref: Map 1, D6)

Off A920, 5 miles NW of Inverurie, Aberdeenshire (signposted).

There are two adjacent monuments at this site. The larger of the two is the recumbent stone circle which

has eight stones as well as the recumbent and flankers. As at most other recumbent stone circles (eg **Easter Aquorthies**) the stones are graded with the lower stones opposite the recumbent. The stone beside the east flanker is decorated with a line of cup marks. A ring cairn was later constructed within the circle (it is associated with 'Beaker' pottery). Next to the circle is a Bronze Age cremation cemetery delineated by a bank and ditch which contained the cremated remains of over 30 individuals placed in urns or small pits.

Access at all reasonable times.
Parking.
Tel: 0131 668 8800   Fax: 0131 668 8888

Lochbuie Stone Circle

NM 618251   LR: 49   (Map ref: Map 1, G3)
Off A849, Lochbuie, 350 yards N of Lochbuie House, Mull.

This circle originally had nine stones – one has been destroyed and replaced by a boulder. Near the circle are three further stones or 'outliers' which may have been used in astronomical observations.

Lundin Links Standing Stones

NO 404027   LR: 59   (Map ref: Map 1, G6)
Off A915, Lundin Links, golf course, Fife.

Three large standing stones, the remains of a stone circle, are a prominent feature of the surrounding landscape. The tallest stone is over 5 m, and the other two are over 4 m. According to folk tradition these are the gravestones of Danish warriors defeated by Macbeth.

Machrie Moor Stone Circles

HS   NR 910324   LR: 69   (Map ref: Map 1, H3)

Off A841, 3 miles N of Blackwaterfoot, Machrie Moor, Arran (signposted).

The moor around the disused Moss Farm has a surprising number of hut circles, field systems, chambered cairns and round cairns, and at least six stone circles. The most obvious site has three sandstone pillars standing up to 5.5 m high with remains of four or five more stones lying around. The other pillar on the moor was one of a circle of at least six stones. The remaining circles are all boulder circles – a setting of four stones which may originally have had additional stones; a double  ring of boulders; a circle of stones, both granite boulders and sandstone slabs, which originally had twelve stones; and a circle of ten boulders, discovered by excavation, which was hidden under a covering of peat.

Access at all reasonable times – involves 1.5 mile walk.
Tel: 0131 668 8800   Fax: 0131 668 8888

Maes Howe Chambered Cairn

HS HY 318128 LR: 6 (Map ref: Map 2)

On A965, 9 miles W of Kirkwall, Orkney (signposted).

The chambered tomb of Maes Howe is a skilfully built and beautifully designed structure which must rank among the finest prehistoric monuments of Europe.

The mound is set on a low earthen platform which is surrounded by a ditch and bank. Entry to the passage is along a low narrow passage its walls incorporating some massive blocks of stone. Just inside the entrance is a recess containing a block of stone which would have sealed the entrance. The passage enters the square chamber midway along one wall and midway along each of the other walls is an entrance to a side chamber. A buttress in each corner supports the corbelling of the roof. The cap is modern as the original capping had been broken, perhaps as early as the twelfth century when Norse visitors entered the tomb adding runic inscriptions and animal carvings to some of the stones. Unfortunately nothing is known of the contents of the tomb.

Open all year: Apr-Sep daily 9.30-6.30; Oct-Mar Mon-Sat 9.30-4.30, Sun 2-4.30 – closed Thu PM and Fri; closed 25/26 Dec & 1-3 Jan.
Exhibition. Gift shop. Tearoom. WC. Car and coach parking. Group concessions. £.
Tel: **01856 761606**

Midhowe Broch

HS   HY 371306   LR: 6   (Map ref: Map 2)
Off B9064, on SW side of island of Rousay, Orkney (signposted).

Midhowe broch occupies a neck of land overlooking Eynhallow Sound. Two ditches, with a wall between them, cut it off from the adjoining land. There are a number of houses around the broch – several more have been destroyed by coastal erosion. The broch is different from the majority of northern brochs, having a gallery at ground level rather than the usual solid-base construction. The gallery was apparently faulty in its design and its outside wall had to be buttressed with vertical slabs. The partitions in the interior were probably constructed in a late phase of use. Other features in the interior include a hearth and a water tank filled by an underground spring.

Access at all reasonable times.
Tel: **0131 668 8800**   Fax: **0131 668 8888**

Midhowe Chambered Cairn

HS   HY 373306   LR: 6   (Map ref: Map 2)
Off B9064, island of Rousay, Orkney (signposted).

Midhowe is a stalled cairn, excavated in the 1930s and
encased in a shed to protect it from the elements. The
exterior of the cairn was decorated by laying the slabs
in opposing angled rows to produce a herringbone
effect. At 23 m the chamber is longer than average and
is divided into twelve compartments by upright stone
slabs. The first few compartments have no shelves but
most of the others are shelved, along their east wall.
The remains of 25 individuals were found in the tomb,
some of which were laid on the benches. A flint knife
and sherds from seven vessels, including 'Unstan'
bowls, were recovered during the excavations.

Access at all reasonable times.
Tel: 0131 668 8800   Fax: 0131 668 8888

Mousa Broch

HS   HU 457236   LR: 4   (Map ref: Map 2)
*Off A970, Island of Mousa, 14 miles S of Lerwick, Shetland
(signposted).*

This is Scotland's best preserved broch, standing to
over 13 m high. The walls slope in slightly towards the
wallhead, giving the building a 'cooling tower' profile.
The doorway is the only external opening. There are
no guard cells at the entrance but three cells lead off
the central courtyard. The stairway winds round the
tower, between the skins of the wall, to the wallhead.
Mousa is the only broch where access to the wallhead
is possible. Two ledges running round the internal wall
probably held wooden floors. The voids, which break

the wall-line in the interior, may have been designed to reduce weight on the lintels and are a feature noted in many brochs. In the courtyard are the remains of a wheelhouse, a secondary construction, probably built around the third century AD.

Open all year – accessible by boat from Sandwick: weather permitting.
Tel: 0131 668 8800   Fax: 0131 668 8888

Mutiny Stones Long Cairn

NT 622590   LR: 67   (Map ref: Map 1, H6)

Off B6355, 4 miles W of Longformacus, Byrecleugh, Borders (track).

The Mutiny Stones is a long cairn, one of a few in this part of Scotland. It is approximately 80 m long and 20 m at the wider east end. Excavations at the end of the nineteenth century and the early part of the twentieth century revealed little, only a section of walling which might be the remains of a chamber. Some cairn stones have been used to build a sheep fank into the mound.

Ness of Burgi Fort

HS   HU 457206   LR: 4   (Map ref: Map 2)

Off A970, 1 mile SW of Sumburgh, Ness of Burgi, Scatness Peninsula, Shetland.

Positioned across the neck of the promontory is a blockhouse similar to that found in association with the broch at **Clickhimin**. The blockhouse is a rectangular block of walling with an entrance passage running through it which has door checks and barholes part of the way along it. The blockhouse is protected by a rampart with a ditch on either side (the pile of stones is excavation debris). The approach to the promontory is dangerous, especially in bad weather.

Access at all reasonable times – access is difficult.
Tel: 0131 668 8800   Fax: 0131 668 8888

Nether Largie Cairns

HS   NR 828979   LR: 55   (Map ref: Map 1, G3)

Off A816, 0.5 miles SW of Kilmartin, Nether Largie, Kilmartin Glen, Argyll (signposted).

Three cairns, known as Nether Largie North [NR 830984], Mid [NR 830983] and South [NR 828979], are part of a large complex of stones and tombs in the Kilmartin Glen. Nether Largie South, excavated in the 1860s, was found to be a chambered cairn. It is the earliest and has an oblong central chamber built with slabs and walling. Three slabs divide the interior into four compartments. Two cists had been inserted into the cairn, but only one is now visible. The two other cairns covered only cists, two in the case of Nether Largie Mid and one in the case of Nether Largie North. The end slab of one of the cists of Nether Largie Mid is

Nether Largie South

Nether Largie North

carved with a cup-mark and axehead carvings. The capstone of Nether Largie North cairn is also carved with axe carvings and at least 40 cupmarks.

Access at all reasonable times.
Explanatory boards. Parking nearby.
Tel: 0131 668 8800   Fax: 0131 668 8888

New and Old Kinord Prehistoric Settlement

NJ 449001   LR: 37   (Map ref: Map 1, E6)

Off A97, 4.5 miles E of Ballater, New Kinord, Dinnet National Nature Reserve, Kincardine and Deeside.

The hut circles known as New Kinord are set within a triangular enclosure. The largest is 19 m in diameter. There is also a souterrain which was accessed from one or two of the huts. A little to the west is a further enclosed group of hut circles. Although there has been some excavation at these sites, it has not been possible to date them closer than the later part of the first millennium BC.

Ord Archaeological Trail

NC 574055   LR: 16   (Map ref: Map 1, C4)

Off A839, The Ord, Lairg, Sutherland (signposted).

The Ord, a low hill overlooking Loch Shin, has the remains of many structures representing settlement from the Neolithic to the post-Medieval period. Near the summit of the hill are two chambered tombs and there are also several later cairns but the most common monument type is the so-called hut-circle, a ring of turf and stone, resulting from the collapse and decay of prehistoric roundhouses. A depression in the bank often indicates the position of the entrance. Hut circles are thought to span the period 1500 BC to the first few centuries AD.

Leaflets for the archaeological trail which winds across the hillside can be obtained from the Centre (or downloaded from www.higharch.demon.co.uk).

There is another archaeological trail at Yarrows, off

the A9 between Lybster and Thrumster, the path of which runs past a broch, round houses and two long cairns.

Access at all reasonable times.
Tel: 01549 402638
Email: archaeology@higharch.demon.co.uk
Web: www.higharch.demon.co.uk

Pettigarth's Field Prehistoric Houses and Cairns

HU 587652   LR: 2   (Map ref: Map 2)
Pettigarth's Field, NE of island of Whalsay, Yoxie Geo, Shetland.

These two houses, known locally as the Benie Hoose and the Standing Stones of Yoxie, were excavated earlier this century. Both are oval in shape and have a passage leading inside from a courtyard. The house higher up the slope is the Benie Hoose which has one room. The Standing Stones of Yoxie has two rooms. Stone tools and pottery were found during the excavations. In addition to the houses are two burial sites, a square cairn with a chamber and a cist covered with a round cairn.

Pobull Fhinn Stone Circle

NF 843650   LR: 18   (Map ref: Map 1, D2)
Off A867, 5 miles W of Lochmaddy, Langass, North Uist.

The Pobull Fhinn stone circle originally had 48 stones. Thirty remain, some of which have fallen. The tallest stone is over 2 m high.

Access at all reasonable times.

Pobull Fhinn

Quoyness Chambered Cairn

HS   HY 677378   LR: 5   (Map ref: Map 2)

Off B9069, 4 miles E of Kettletoft, Island of Sanday, Orkney (footpath).

Quoyness is a Maes Howe tomb (see **Maes Howe**). The entrance passage was originally 9 m long but is now roofed for only about 3 m as the exterior around the entrance has been reconstructed to show the construction of the cairn. The chamber is rectangular and has six cells leading off it – two off each of the long walls and one off each of the short walls. The chamber walls are vertical to about 1 m then converge for a further 3 m to the reconstructed roof. During excavations in the 1860s human bones were found in four of the cells and in a cist dug into the chamber floor.

Access at all reasonable time – torch required.
Tel: 0131 668 8800   Fax: 0131 668 8888

Rennibister Souterrain

HS   HY 397125   LR: 6   (Map ref: Map 2)

Off A965, 3 miles W of Kirkwall, Rennibister, Orkney (signposted).

The souterrain at Rennibister Farm was discovered in 1926 when its roof gave way beneath the wheels of a steam tractor. Originally, entry into the souterrain would have been by crawling along a low passage from a house above the ground, but now entry is through a hatch in the roof and down a ladder. The chamber is oval, its corbelled roof supported by pillars. Five recesses were built into the chamber walls. When the chamber was cleared, the remains of at least eighteen individuals were found – it is rare for human bones to be found in an earth-house, and it is possible that the earth-house was used as a burial vault when its domestic use was over.

Access at all reasonable times.
Tel: 0131 668 8800   Fax: 0131 668 8888

Ring of Brodgar Circle and Henge

HS   HY 294134   LR: 6   (Map ref: Map 2)

On B9055, 5 miles NE of Stromness, Orkney.

The Ring of Brodgar is one of the largest stone circles in Scotland (36 stones out of an original total of 60 remain, some up to 4.5 m high). The site comprises a stone circle surrounded by a ditch (there is no trace of the bank). The ditch was originally up to 3 m deep and 9 m across and is crossed by two causeways in the north-west and the south-east. The Ring of Brodgar may have been part of a 'ritual complex' which included **Maes Howe** and the **Stones of Stenness**. No

excavations have been carried out in the interior so the rituals associated with the circle can only be guessed at. On one of the broken stones in the northern section of the circle, a Norse visitor to the site has carved runes and a cross.

Access at all reasonable times.
Parking.
Tel: 0131 668 8800   Fax: 0131 668 8888

Rubh' an Dunain Cairn and Dun

NG 393163   LR: 32   (Map ref: Map 1, E2)
Off B8009, 4 miles S of Glenbrittle, Rubh' an Dunain, Skye.

The chambered tomb at Rubh' an Dunain is a round cairn with a concave forecourt. The facade, chamber and passage were constructed using alternate pillars and panels of drystone walling and the kerb retaining the cairn material may also have been built in this way. The passage, which is roofed with large stones, leads into a polygonal chamber which is now roofless. When the cairn was excavated in the 1930s, pottery and flint artefacts were recovered. The bones of several individuals were recovered, including some which dated to reuse of the tomb in the early Bronze Age. Near the tomb are the remains of an Iron Age promontory fort.

Scatness Broch and Settlement

HU 390106   LR: 4   (Map ref: Map 2)

On A970, 0.5 miles NW of Sumburgh, Scatness, Shetland.

The site at Scatness provides a chance to visit an ongoing excavation. Archaeologists are investigating a broch (up to 5 m appears to be standing) and its surrounding settlement, some of which post-dates the broch and includes Norse occupation. One of the buildings was reused by the Vikings as a smithy – this building has been reconstructed near to the site.

Scord of Brouster Prehistoric Settlement

HU 255516   LR: 3   (Map ref: Map 2)

Off A971, 1.5 miles NW of Bridge of Walls, Scord of Brouster, on the ground above Brouster Farm, Shetland.

The stone walls of the settlement at Scord of Brouster stand out clearly from the hillside. Excavations carried out in some areas of the site in the 1930s included investigations at the house adjacent to the enclosure nearest the road. Material recovered allowed its period of use to be radiocarbon dated to 3000 to 2500 BC. The house has an oval central area, in the middle of which was a hearth, and partitions dividing the area around the walls into six.

Scottish Crannog Centre (Kenmore)

NN 772453   LR: 51   (Map ref: Map 1, G5)

Off A827, 6 miles W of Aberfeldy, Kenmore, Perthshire.

Off the A827, 12 km W of Aberfeldy, Perthshire.
The reconstructed crannog at Kenmore is based on
research carried out at Oakbank crannog near Fearnan
which dated to the late Bronze Age/early Iron Age.

There is not much to see in visiting most crannog sites – usually all that is left is a stony islet and many are at least semi-submerged – so this is a good chance to see what a crannog would have looked like when it was occupied. The Kenmore crannog was built by hand and the skills of the crannog builders are apparent in the reconstruction. On the shore in the Crannog Centre there is an exhibition which explores the way of life of the people who lived in the crannogs and a video explaining how the crannog was built and how archaeologists research underwater sites.

Open daily Apr-Oct, 10.00-17.30.
Exhibition. Audio-visual presentation. Guided tour. Hands-on craft demonstrations. Group bookings and school parties welcome. Gift/Refreshment kiosk. Disabled access. Parking. £
Tel: 01887 830583   Fax: 01887 380876
Email: info@crannog.co.uk   Web: www.crannog.co.uk

Skara Brae Neolithic Settlement

HS   HY 231188   LR: 6   (Map ref: Map 2)
Off B9056, 7 miles N of Stromness, Orkney (signposted).

The famous Neolithic village of Skara Brae was excavated by V. G. Childe in the 1920s. The sand was removed to reveal a group of remarkably well preserved stone-built houses connected by low passages. In the centre of each hut is a rectangular, kerbed hearth. Stone 'box beds' and dressers were uncovered, and there were storage places built into the walls. The excavated houses can only be viewed from the path above but a reconstructed house beside the visitor centre can be entered and explored. The visitor centre displays some of the bone and stone artefacts and pottery, including highly decorated 'Grooved Ware',

which was recovered during the excavations. It also features interactive displays and an audio-visual presentation telling the story of the village and its people.

Open all year: Apr-Sep, daily 9.30-18.30; Oct-Mar, Mon-Sat 9.30-16.30, Sun 14.00-16.30; closed 25/26 Dec & 1-3 Jan.
Visitor centre. Gift shop. Cafe. WC. Disabled Access. Parking. ££. Joint ticket with Skail House (in summer) and a joint ticket for entry to Orkney monuments (HS) is also available.
Tel: 01856 841815   Fax: 01856 841885

Stanydale Prehistoric Settlement

HS   HU 285502   LR: 3   (Map ref: Map 2)
Off A971, 2 miles SE of Bridge of Walls, Stanydale, Shetland (signposted/path).

The walk to the so-called Stanydale Temple passes an excavated and partially reconstructed house which puts the scale of the 'temple' into perspective. The 'temple' has a crescent facade with an entrance through two doors (their positions marked by checks) leading into an oval room much larger than that of the house. In the middle of the room are two large postholes which would have held the posts supporting the roof. The inner part of the building, opposite the doorway, has a number of alcoves, some of which had hearths. Most domestic buildings have a central hearth and this, coupled with the scale of the building, suggests that it had a different function, perhaps as a meeting place for the community.

Access at all reasonable times – the path to the site from the road is marked by posts.
Tel: 0131 668 8800   Fax: 0131 668 8888

Stones of Stenness and Henge

HS   HY 306126   LR: 6   (Map ref: Map 2)
On B9055, 5 miles NE of Stromness, Orkney.

Only four stones of this circle remain out of twelve. A ditch, originally over 2 m deep, surrounds the stone circle and was crossed by one causeway. The site was

excavated in the 1970s and a stone setting was uncovered in the centre of the circle. Animal bones found in the ditch were interpreted as the remains of feasting or sacrifice at the henge. Radiocarbon dates obtained from the material recovered during the excavations indicate that the circle was of a similar date to the nearby settlement at **Barnhouse**.

Access at any reasonable time.
Parking.
Tel: 0131 668 8800   Fax: 0131 668 8888

Strontoiller Cairn and Standing Stones

NM 907289   LR: 49   (Map ref: Map 1, G3)
Off A816, 3 miles E of Oban, S of Strontoiller farm, Argyll.

The standing stone at Strontoiller is a rough-cut pillar, standing 4 m high. Traditionally it is said to mark the grave of Diarmid, the Irish mythical hero. The adjacent cairn was excavated in the 1960s and found to have been opened previously. A scatter of cremated bone was found in the centre of the cairn. Quartz chips and pebbles were found under the kerbstones of the cairn. Quartz is often associated with burial sites in the west, and was probably ritually scattered during construction of the tomb.

Sunhoney Stone Circle

NJ 715056   LR: 38   (Map ref: Map 1, E6)
Off B9119, 5.5 miles N of Banchory, Sunhoney farm, Aberdeenshire (track).

The circle at Sunhoney, now surrounded by trees, has eleven standing stones and a recumbent stone. The recumbent is of grey granite and the uprights are of red granite. The recumbent has probably fallen over. What is now its upper face is decorated with 30 cupmarks. There is a ring cairn within the circle.

Tap o' Noth Fort

NJ 484293   LR: 37   (Map ref: Map 1, D6)

Off A97 or A941, 1.5 miles NW of Rhynie, Tap o' Noth, Aberdeenshire (track).

The Tap o' Noth fort is perched on top of a high hill. A massive timber-laced stone rampart, originally up to 8 m

thick, surrounds the summit and there is a further rampart lower down the hill. Up to 150 hut platforms pepper the interior of the fort – some of them may be quarry scoops dug out during the construction of the ramparts.

Taversoe Tuick Chambered Cairn

HS HY 426276 LR: 6 (Map ref: Map 2)
On B9065, island of Rousay, Orkney (signposted).

Taversoe Tuick is an unusual double-storey chambered tomb, discovered during gardening work at Trumland House. The chambers were not linked and had indi-

vidual entrances. The lower chamber is cut into the rock. Upright slabs divide it into four compartments, each of which contain flagstone shelves. Piles of bones were found in the chamber. The upper chamber is divided in two and contained cremated remains in three stone cists. Near the cairn is a smaller chamber 1.5 m long dug into the ground, which is divided into five by slabs. Pottery bowls were recovered, but no skeletal remains.

Access at all reasonable times.
Tel: 0131 668 8800 Fax: 0131 668 8888

Temple Wood Stone Circles

HS   NR 826978   LR: 55   (Map ref: Map 1, G3)

Off A816, 1 mile S of Kilmartin, Temple Wood, Kilmartin Glen, Argyll.

The site at Temple Wood comprises a circle of stones 12 m in diameter. Two of the stones are decorated, one with two concentric circles, the other with a double spiral. Excavations in the 1970s revealed that before the stone

circle was constructed, there was an earlier circle nearby, first timber, then stone, now marked by a ring of posts. Burials, in small cairns and cists, in and around the stone circle, indicate its use over centuries. The circle was eventually covered by the stones of a large cairn.

The museum at **Kilmartin House** has information on the archaeological monuments of the area and can provide information on an archaeological trail which includes Temple Wood.

Access at all reasonable times.
Parking nearby.
Tel: 0131 668 8800   Fax: 0131 668 8888

Tinto Hill Cairn

NS 953343   LR: 72   (Map ref: Map 1, H5)
Off A73, 5.5 miles SW of Biggar, Tinto Hill, Lanarkshire (footpath).

The cairn on the summit of Tinto Hill is one of the largest Bronze Age round cairns in Scotland. It measures 45 m in diameter and is nearly 6 m high. From the summit of the hill are extensive views of the Clyde Valley and the Southern Uplands.

Tirefour Broch

NM 867429   LR: 49   (Map ref: Map 1, G3)
Off B8045, 2 miles NE of Achnacroish, Lismore (track).

Tirefour broch still stands to 5 m on one side. It has additional defences across the ridge on two sides. In the interior the scarcement and the galleries within the wall can be seen.

Tomnaverie Stone Circle

HS   NJ 48○○○   LR: 37   (Map ref: Map 1, E6)
On B9094, 3.5 miles NW of Aboyne, Aberdeenshire.

The red granite circle at Tomnaverie is 18 m in diameter – four of its stones and the whinstone recumbent remain in place. Within the circle is a ring of smaller stones, the kerb of a ring cairn. There are extensive views to Lochnagar and the Cairngorms from the site.

Access at all reasonable times.
Tel: 0131 668 8800   Fax: 0131 668 8888

Torhouse Stone Circle

HS   NX 382565   LR: 83   (Map ref: Map 1, J4)

Off B733, 3.5 miles W of Wigtown, Torhouse, Dumfries and Galloway (signposted).

The circle at Torhouse has 19 granite boulders, graded in height with the largest boulder, weighing some six tons, situated in the south-east. In the middle of the circle are three stones, two large ones with a smaller one between which may indicate a link with the recumbent stone circles of the north-east (eg **Sunhoney**).

Access at all reasonable times.
Tel: 0131 668 8800   Fax: 0131 668 8888

Torwoodlee Fort and Broch

NT 475381   LR: 73   (Map ref: Map 1, H6)

Off A72, 2 miles NW of Galashiels, Torwoodlee, Borders (track).

The broch at Torwoodlee survives to less than 1 m in height. In the entrance passage the door check is visible. A door off the courtyard leads to a cell and the stairway within the wall. The broch is built on the site of an earlier fort which is now difficult to detect. One hypothesis is that it was demolished by the Romans.

Traprain Law Fort

NT 581746   LR: 67   (Map ref: Map 1, H6)

Off A1, 2 miles SE of East Linton, Traprain Law, East Lothian (footpath).

The summit of Traprain Law has two main ramparts, clearest along the north and west of the hill. A large part of the north-east of the hill has been removed by

quarrying. Excavations have been carried out on the summit and artefacts dating from the Neolithic to the Early Historic period were recovered. A large collection of late Roman silver (now in the Museum of Scotland, Edinburgh) was found under the floor of one of the many houses dotted around the summit.

Twelve Apostles Stone Circle

NX 947794   LR: 84   (Map ref: Map 1, I5)

Off A76 or B729, 3 miles NW of Dumfries, Newbridge, Dumfries and Galloway.

Eleven stones now survive in the 'Twelve Apostles' stone circle, although it is thought that there were originally 18 stones. The circle is the largest in Scotland and one of the largest in Britain, measuring almost 87 m at its widest point. Four of the stones are boulders and the remainder were quarried.

Access at all reasonable times.
Parking.

Tynron Doon

NX 819939   LR: 78   (Map ref: Map 1, I5)

Off A702, 3.5 miles NE of Moniaive, Achengibbert Hill, Tynron Doon, Dumfries and Galloway.

The ramparts of Tynron Doon which defend the western slopes can be seen clearly from the approach to the hill. There are three ramparts separated by deep ditches and a drystone wall around the summit. The outlines of a number of hut circles can be made out within the enclosure. Finds from the site show that the fort was used from the Iron Age until relatively recently – an L-shaped tower house was built in the enclosure, probably in the late sixteenth century.

Unival Chambered Cairn

NF 800667   LR: 18   (Map ref: Map 1, D1)

Off A865, 1.5 miles N of Claddach Illeray, S of Unival, North Uist.

This square cairn has been greatly robbed of its stone and the most obvious remaining features are the upright stones which lined the forecourt, passage and chamber walls. The tallest slabs (2.5 m) are at the entrance to the passage. The site was excavated in the 1930s. A cist containing burnt human bone fragments was found in one corner. Round the walls of the chamber were piles of mixed bone and pottery, perhaps indicating that the contents of the cist were emptied out between burials.

Unstan Chambered Cairn

HS   HY 283117   LR: 6   (Map ref: Map 2)

Off A965, 3 miles NE of Stromness, Unstan, Orkney (signposted).

The chambered cairn of Unstan is situated on a promontory in the Loch of Stenness. It was excavated in the

1850s and is now capped by a modern concrete dome. The mound was built of concentric rings of drystone walling around the central chamber. A long passage leads into the chamber which is divided by upright slabs into stalls. A side cell leads off the central chamber. Skeletal remains were recovered from each compartment and from the side cell. Animal and bird bones were also recovered as well as sherds from at least 30 shallow bowls with wide collars which were sometimes decorated. This pottery, known as 'Unstan Ware' has now been found at a number of funerary and domestic sites in Orkney and further afield.

Access at all reasonable times.
Tel: 0131 668 8800   Fax: 0131 668 8888

Wag of Forse Broch and Settlement

ND 204352   LR: 11   (Map ref: Map1, C5)

Off A9 or A895, 1 mile NW of Latheron, Forse, Caithness (track).

The site at Forse was excavated in 1930s and 1940s, uncovering a turf-walled enclosure with the remains of a succession of houses of different styles. The first houses on the site were small roundhouses. The next building on the site was a large circular building with some features similar to brochs including a cell and stretch of gallery with a stair. The 'broch' was succeeded by rectangular buildings – 'wags' – with stone pillars inside which would presumably have supported lintel stones. One, to the west of the broch, is 12 m long and has the remains of two rows of stone pillars.

Wideford Hill Chambered Cairn

HS   HY 409122   LR: 6   (Map ref: Map 2)

Off A965, 2 miles W of Kirkwall, Wideford Hill, Orkney (signposted).

Wideford Hill chambered cairn is similar in layout to the chambered cairns at **Maes Howe** and **Quoyness**, having a rectangular chamber with three side-cells leading off it, one of which is cut into the bedrock. Entry to the chamber was originally through a long, low passage but is now through a trapdoor in the roof and down a ladder.

Access at all reasonable times – involves a long walk.
Tel: 0131 668 8800   Fax: 0131 668 8888

Midmar Recumbent Stone Circle

Dunchraigaig Cairn, Kilmartin Glen

a Wee Guide to
Prehistoric
Scotland

Museums

Museums

Aberdeen Anthropological Museum

Marischal College, Broad Street, Aberdeen.

Open all year: Mon-Fri 10.00-17.00, Sun 14.00-17.00.
Temporary exhibitions. WC. Parties welcome but must
book. Parking nearby. Free admission.
Tel: 01224 274301

Bute Museum

Off A845, Stuart Street, Rothesay, Bute.

**Open all year: Apr-Sep, Mon-Sat 10.30-16.30, Sun
14.30-16.30; Oct-Mar, Tue-Sat 14.30-16.30; closed Sun
& Mon.**
Guided tours by appt. Explanatory displays. Gift shop.
WC. Disabled access and assistance. £.
Tel: 01700 502033

Dumfries Museum & Camera Obscura

The Observatory, Church Street, Dumfries.

**Open all year, Mon-Sat 10.00-13.00 & 14.00-17.00, Sun
14.00-17.00; closed Sun & Mon Oct-Mar; camera
obscura closed Oct-Mar.**
Tel: 01387 253374   Fax: 01387 265081

Glasgow Art Gallery and Museum

Kelvingrove, Glasgow.

Open all year, Mon-Sat 10.00-17.00, Sun 11.00-17.00; closed 25/26 Dec & 1/2 Jan.
Parking. Gift shop. Cafe. WC. Disabled access. Free admission.
Tel: 0141 287 2699   Fax: 0141 287 2690

Hunterian Museum

University of Glasgow, Glasgow.

Open all year, Mon-Sat 9.30-17.00; closed certain Public Holidays: phone to confirm.
Gift shop. Cafe. WC. Free admission.
Tel: 0141 330 4221   Fax: 0141 330 3617

Huntly House Museum

142 Canongate, Royal Mile, Edinburgh.

Open all year Mon-Sat 10.00-18.00 (during Festival Sun 14.00-17.00)
Gift shop. WC. Free admission.
Tel: 0131 529 4143   Fax: 0131 529 3977

Inverness Museum and Art Gallery

Castle Wynd, Inverness.

Open all year, Mon-Sat 9.00-17.00; closed public hols.
Explanatory displays. Gift shop. Restaurant. WC. Disabled access. Parking nearby. Free admission
Tel: 01463 237114   Fax: 01463 225293

McManus Galleries

Off A85, Albert Square, Dundee.

Open all year: Mon-Sat 10.00-16.00, Thu 10.00-19.00, Sun 12.30-16.00; closed 25/26 Dec & 1-2 Jan.
Guided tours by arrangement. Exhibitions. Gift shop. Cafe. WC. Disabled access. Parking nearby. Free admission.
Tel: 01382 432084   Fax: 01382 432052

Museum nan Eilean, Stornoway

Francis Street, Stornoway, Lewis.

Open all year: Apr-Sep, Mon-Sat 10.00-17.30; Oct-Nov, Tue-Fri 10.00-17.00, Sat 10.00-13.00.
Explanatory displays. WC. Limited disabled access. Parking nearby.
Tel: 01851 703773 x266   Fax: 01851 706318
Email: rlanghome@w-isles.gov.uk

Museum of Scotland

Chambers Street, Edinburgh.

Open all year Mon-Sat 10.00-17.00, Tue 10.00-20.00, Sun 12.00-17.00; closed 25 Dec
Museum. Gift shop. Audio guides. Tearooms. WC. Disabled access & WC. Parking nearby. £
Tel: 0131 247 4422   Fax: 0131 220 4819

Orkney Museum

Tankerness House, Broad Street, Kirkwall, Orkney.

Open all year: Apr-Sep, Mon-Sat 10.30-17.00; Oct-Mar, Mon-Sat 10.30-12.30 & 13.30-17.00 (May-Sep Sun 14.00-17.00).
Guided tours by arrangement. Exhibitions. Gift shop. Garden. WC. Disabled access. Parking nearby. Free admission.
Tel: 01856 873191   Fax: 01856 871560

Perth Museum and Art Gallery

George Street, Perth.

Open all year Mon-Sat 10-17.00; closed Christmas & New Year.
Exhibitions. Gift shop. Disabled access. WC. Car parking. Free admission.
Tel: 01738 632488   Fax: 01738 443505

Shetland Museum

Lower Hillhead, Lerwick, Shetland.

Open all year: Mon, Wed & Fri 10.00-19.00, Tue, Thu & Sat 10.00-17.00.
Exhibitions. Gift shop. WC. Disabled access (lift) & WC. Parking nearby. Free admission.
Tel: 01595 695057 Fax: 01595 696729

Thurso Heritage Museum

Town Hall, High Street, Thurso.

Open Jun-Sep, Mon-Sat 10.00-13.00 & 14.00-17.00.
Guided tours on request. Exhibitions. WC. Disabled
access. Car and coach parking. £.
Tel: 01847 892692

Index